The Last of the Breed
The Story of Trapper Jake Korell

Jake Korell

As Told to Kit Collings

ISBN 0-7414-2843-1

Published by:

INFI∞ITY
PUBLISHING.COM

1094 New Dehaven Street, Suite 100
West Conshohocken, PA 19428-2713
Info@buybooksontheweb.com
www.buybooksontheweb.com
Toll-free (877) BUY BOOK
Local Phone (610) 941-9999
Fax (610) 941-9959

Printed in the United States of America

Printed on Recycled Paper

Published November 2005

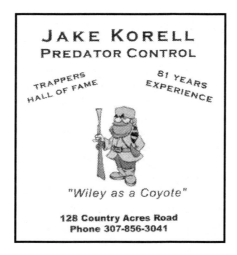

JAKE KORELL
PREDATOR CONTROL

TRAPPERS
HALL OF FAME

81 YEARS
EXPERIENCE

"Wiley as a Coyote"

128 Country Acres Road
Phone 307-856-3041

Table of Contents

Author Information

Kit Collings lives in western Wyoming and has been a published writer since 1976 specializing in Wyoming history. Collings has been the membership chair for Western Writers of America.

Acknowledgments

We would like to thank the following who helped with this project, Lew Diehl, Ted Knowles, Jerry Korell, Gary Shoop, Jim James, Tom Krause, Lee Teter, Jane Maller, Loren Jost and the Wind River Heritage Center.

Proceeds from the sale of this book go to:

Wind River Heritage Center
P.O. Box 206 ~ 412 Fremont Avenue
Riverton, Wyoming 82501
307-856-0706

Cover

The cover is a bronze of Jake Korell by sculptor Gary Shoop of Riverton, Wyoming. The sculpture was commissioned by Dr. Harmon Keyes of Phoenix, AZ who is a friend of Korell's. It not only depicts Jake's lifetime – since Jake trapped since he was seven years old; but also depicts a colorful part of the making of the West. It is named "Jake/1985". It portrays Jake on snowshoes with traps in hand and carrying a rifle. The bronze is an exact likeness of Jake running his trap lines in his badger coat, leather leggings, and beaver cap. (Cover picture courtesy of Gary Shoop)

Sculptor Gary Shoop (left) with Jake Korell and his bronze statute.

Dedication

The book is dedicated to Martha, Jake's beloved wife, who died from illness during the writing of this book.

Chapter One – Introduction

Sitting by the campfire at the remote Watkins Camp in the Dunoir Valley with veteran trapper Jake Korell is a treat. The sunset is reflecting a soft orange on Kisinger Lakes and the spectacular spires of Pinnacle Buttes. High in the sky Northern Geese were practicing their formation flying in preparation for their long southerly flight. The Dunoir is a glaciated volcanic valley of high plateaus between lush open meadows near the continental divide in northwest Wyoming. Jake's blue eyes start to sparkle with mischief and a slight smile starts and then is gone so fast that you think you are mistaken as he starts to tell a story. And Jake has stories!! Jake is known as a colorful character with a wonderful sense of humor. He has trapped, fished and hunted since he was six or seven. The slightly built man pours campfire coffee for all of us and serves the cutthroat trout that was caught today. Jake's special way of wrapping the fish with a couple strips of bacon before enclosing it in tin foil to cook in the coals of the campfire made the meal he'd cooked outstandingly scrumptious.

Jake Korell in an elk skin leather shirt made for him by Paul Throckmartin. He is a rugged Wyoming individual with a true zest for life. Jake's been trapping since 1921 and is planning where he will trap next winter. Korell has collected a variety of traps, hides and has given many historic items to the Wind River Heritage Museum in Riverton, Wyoming, along with a collection of virtually every Wyoming animal. These are not just head mounts but the complete animal is mounted in a natural stance.

2

Grocery Wreck

Korell was close to the campfire site for this story. "I used to do a lot of hunting and guiding in this area," Jake smirks, "and one time I almost lost my life. Jerry and I were back by Pendergraft Peak, there was a black bear. When the dudes got there to go hunting the next day the bear had chewed all the canned stuff full of holes. He took a crap on the table and tore the flour sacks open. So the dudes didn't have any food. The bear even tore a great big slit in the tent. And so my son, Jerry, and I came out to get more groceries. On the way back we were each taking pack string up to Pendergraft Peak to where the hunters were waiting for us. I was leading a pack horse named Cherry, a sorrel, an ornery thing and a big 1300 pound mule was tied behind him. We went north past Brooks Lake and the animals acted like they were thirsty so we stopped at a stream to drink.

"Nearby an old rancher from Dubois, Ab Cross, was punching cows and never went anywhere without a 45 revolver strapped on to him. He was kind of a character; if he liked you he would do anything for you, but if he didn't you better stay out of his way.

"The horse wasn't leading too good so I had a dally on the horn. My ropes were wet because it was in the morning and there was frost on them.

"The mule came forward to drink and the lead rope came under the Cherry horse's tail. Cherry started abuckin' a circle around me. I was trying to get down under that rope so it would go on over the top of me. It wouldn't turn loose.

"The horse was bucking and the mule was pulling back and kicking me and tightening the rope around me. Tried to get under the lead rope but it was wrapped around me three or four times and I was between the mule and the horse. I was jerked out of the saddle. My arm was penned in and I couldn't get my knife. I was hanging and could not touch the ground.

Jake and animal display at Jake's trading Post in 1993. His friend, Lew Diehl observed, "Jake works very hard at what he is doing (he has been known to play very hard also). He believes in being committed to a project and being persistent until the job is done. Jake is also very conservative and spends and invests his income as wisely as possible. If Jake has a weakness, it is going to auctions. He usually finds some traps or equipment which can be bought very reasonably. He just might need it some day. Please enjoy his life story and learn to know Jake as I do. This is a marvelous study in human lifestyle. Jake is a self starter who doesn't sit around and cry when things go wrong. Jake worked very hard, always tried to please his employers and customers."

"Jerry looked back and he come agallopin'. Ab rode over and pulled his 45 and was going to kill the horse to save my life. Jerry beat him to it and yelled, 'got it' just as Ab was just ready to pull the trigger. With a sharp knife my son chopped the rope in two and I hit the ground. The knife went thru the rope and slit the horse's rump which was bleeding as he bolted up the hill.

"That was the last thing I remember as I hit the ground and blacked out. The mule just stood there after the other horse left. Couldn't hardly get the rope off it was wrapped so tight. My stomach was tightened into a six inch circle. When I come to they helped me up on the horse. Jerry led the horse and Ab held me on as I was about ready to pass out again as they took me to Brooks Lake Lodge which was about a mile away.

"Back up to the lodge they put me to bed, so sick that they couldn't move me for two days. They brought a doctor in. Tore all my ribs loose. Couldn't do much trapping that year. Took me all winter to heal up. Close one – just about cut me in two. That was a close one.

"I walked lopsided for a while, one hip was 2"-3" higher than the other. The more active I done the better it got. It straightened out. I'm plumb normal now."

"One evening a few days later, Jerry was out hunting with the dudes. A little before dark they returned to camp and the same bear came out of the cook tent. Jerry jumped off his horse and the bear was agallopin' straight away and my son nailed him. Jerry sold the bear's hide to one of the dudes for a hella of a price."

Two Elk

On a lighter note Jake started another tale. "An interesting story happened in 1964 on the Pinnacles Trail," Korell stated as he gestured toward the path. "Towards evening while riding off of this bench near here with these guys that only had two days left in their hunt. I heard some elk sound, slid off my horse dropped and told the guys to stay with the horses. The elk kept bugling as I crawled up beside an old rotten log. I saw there were both a cow and a bull. I killed the cow but the bull didn't seem to know where the shot had come from. He came running right at me. I didn't know he was that close and he didn't know I was there. He jumped over the top of the log I was hiding behind as I pumped in a shell and I don't even remember shooting as the bull leaped over me. The bullet went through the jaw from below and up into his brain.

"I was sore and all black and blue from where his hoofs had landed on me and my shirt was torn. He went end over end and broke off his two brow points. My gun was kinda scarred up, too. I went over to where I thought he had run and sure enough he was there. So I filled both of their licenses right there."

Long Shot

Jake sat down and stroked his beard before continuing. "That was the shortest shot I ever made, but the longest shot was when Tommy Knight and a couple of movie directors were near Buffalo Fort. I saw a spike standing on a knob. We were riding down the trail and I was on a fast roping horse—a bronc. He was about a five year old and I didn't have him broke good. But he was real tired. When I stopped he put his head down and I wrapped the reins on the horn. Pulled my 270 Remington rifle out real slow. I knew if I stepped off that spike would just take off and be out of sight. He just stood there. I got the gun around and I got it on him. I pulled the trigger and the horse come awake. Things happened. He bucked all the way down. I threw my gun away and grabbed for leather. I finally got him rode. I rode back and picked up my rifle and wiped it off. It had a few nicks on it. I asked the guys if I had gotten him. They didn't know for he had gone out of sight when I pulled the trigger. We rode over and there he lay. We walked it out and it was over 653 yards."

Jake laid out a trail straight to the Pinnacles and it is still known as Jake's trail. Jake has a wonderful sense of humor and a keen wit. He loves to share his personal experience and stories with anyone who will listen. He has had over 84 years of successful trapping. This is his story, his wisdom and his stories.

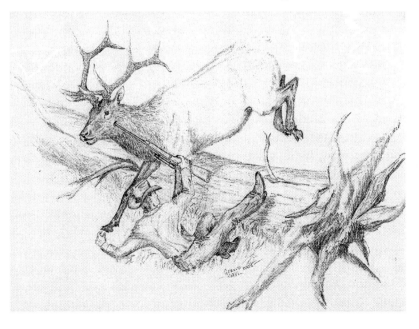

Chapter Two -- How it all Started – with Pocket Gophers, Muskrats and Skunks

Jake starts to play his harmonica by the campfire. The notes of *Red Wing* and then *Red River Valley* have both a light and haunting tone in this mountain top cathedral.

Family History

Jake (Jacob) Korell was born on April 22, 1914, in Lincoln Nebraska. His ancestors migrated from Germany to Russia when Catherine the Great promised them rich farm land. Jake's parents were born in Russia. Jake's father, Henry, was inducted into the Russian army's band and became a drummer for them. Although he had been discharged he was suppose to stay in the reserves until 1922. He went AWOL and took a ship, along with his wife, Elizabeth, and children Mary, Katherine, and Henry bound for America. Due to the confusion and/or language barrier, they got on the wrong ship and wound up in Buenos Aires, Argentina, for four years before raising enough money to continue on to Ellis Island in New York.

Jake Korell's Parents, Elizabeth (Ernst) Korell and Heinrich "Henry" Jaconlich Korell, taken in 1929 in Lingle, Wyoming. Jake's father was a good provider for he worked roundhouse in Lincoln, Nebraska, in winter, carpentered, ranched and farmed sugar beets in summer along with the whole family.

The family's language, customs and culture remained German. The family migrated to Lincoln, Nebraska, in 1911 where they tended sugar beets. At home they only spoke German as his mother never learned English and his father just butchered it. (He would compose his sentences with the subject last as is done in German.) Nine children were born to this family. The oldest son, Henry died in a wagon accident and so the unborn son was named Henry and called Henry II.

Lingle school house

There were about 150,000 people in Wyoming when the family eventually settled on the old John Burns Ranch near Lingle, Wyoming. Many Germans from Russia also settled in that area. Lingle lies along the Oregon Trail where mountain men, pony express riders, cavalrymen and pioneers had traveled.

Jake Korell's Parents and Siblings: Henry and Elizabeth Korell and children (left to right, 2nd row): Mary Korell Greenwald, Katherine Korell Knoll; (1st row) Henry Korell I (died at age 6 when wagon box fell on him), John Korell, Pauline Korell Frank (baby). Top row is Elizabeth's sister and her husband. Four more children were born after this photo was taken: Jake Korell in 1914, Rose Korell Wells, Henry Korell II and Eddie Korell. (Jake was just a glint in his fathers eye at the time the picture was taken.).

The family farmed sugar beets with sharp shod big horses that went over high beet dumps. Jake would crawl along the beet row behind the hoer blocking the beets. Korell would thin them as shown in the sketch on the left. Jake's brother who was four years older, was the best beet scooper Jake ever knew. He could scoop 6 tons on the wagon faster than anyone in our family including my uncles. He was 5' 6" tall and weighed 165 pounds with big arms. Lingle had the largest sugar beet loading station in Wyoming.

Jake was asked by his first grade teacher to read to all the grades – even the big kids. He read with so much expression that everyone enjoyed his readings.

Jake was the 6th child of nine. He did not like the farming part as much as the ranching. Jake always liked horses. He enjoyed breaking saddle horses and riding them.

Jake's Early Trapping

At the age of seven Jake started trapping pocket gophers that were damaging the fields. Also his father, brothers, and uncles showed him how to trap and hunt.

Hiram D. Lingle had a lot of land on Rawhide Creek and hired a bunch of kids when Jake was nine or ten years old. He gave us each a dozen gopher traps. The gophers were doing a lot of damage in the crops or when they dug their hole in the middle of an irrigation ditch the water would follow their hole and come out in the middle of the field and wash the whole thing out. When you were mowing hay, the sickles would run into the gopher mounds and plug up.

Lingle hired quite a number of kids but Jake got more gophers than the others. Jake would set a trap for a gopher by pushing around with a little steel rod until he found where the main entrance was and then started raking it off with a little scraper. Back about every eight to ten inches where the hole divided into a "Y", he pushed in the gopher trap and left it open. In about 15 minutes the gopher wouldn't want the daylight in there. He would come pushing a load of dirt ahead of him and there was a little plate on the gut-hook trap and when the dirt hit

the plate his belly was about even with hook that kills him. And 15 minutes later you would have his mate. Jake was paid 10 cents for each gopher and netting 30 to 40 a day making the daily sum of $3 - $4 during the '20s when hired hands were earning a dollar a day and board. "I was making more than the hands" Jake chuckled. "Trapped every year since but only did the gophers for a couple of years."

A bonus on the Burns Ranch was the owner, John who lived on the other end of the place and taught Jake all about trapping.

Additionally, Roy Hyer one of his father's ranch hands taught Jake about beaver trapping and how to make lures. A neighbor, Mr. Shawles, showed Jake how to trap

John and Effie Burns

muskrats when he was nine. Korell caught between 20 and 30 muskrats daily and each brought between $1.00 to $1.25. This helped to feed a family of nine children. (Jake's father would "borrow" his trapping money and never pay it back.) Using a leaky boat Jake trapped along both sides of the Rawhide Creek which dumped into the Platte River.

The Rawhide got its name when a wagon train passed through the area in June of 1849 on the way to the gold fields of California. A young man in the train, having vowed to kill the first Indian he saw, shot a maiden. Naturally, the Indians were quite upset about this turn of events. They demanded that he be turned over to them. The wagon party refused. The Indians attacked and then unexpectedly had withdrawn with wild war-whoops when the young man had given himself up to save the train. The Indians skinned him alive, thus the naming of nearby Rawhide Creek and Rawhide Buttes.

Jake trapped on both sides of the creek and the river. In the summer time the water was high and the muskrats had a row of dens up high and in the fall the river was lower and the muskrats made them a new row of holes in the bank. Most of the time Jake set the trap in the slides where the muskrats were going in and out of the water or right in their den if there was den about even with the water. He would use a drown set and stake it on the down side of the hole and that swift water would drown him when he got in that trap. If Jake didn't set it so the muskrat would drown the 'rat would ring his front foot off. In the still water Jake weighted the traps a little. Jake didn't cut the hide when skinning.

Jake when he was boxing professionally as Jackie Karell.

Martha Gradwohl in 1933 at age 16. She came from a family that also spoke German.

Muskrats are cased and fleshed most of the fat fleshed off, and turned flesh side out until he's dry and then he's ready for sale. The ermine or weasels (called weasels in the summer and ermines in the winter when they're white) live in the high holes. Ermine brought $3.00 apiece.

The Korell family would sit around and play music in the evenings. Everyone was musically inclined. Two of the girls played piano and Jake and his brother played the accordion. Jake also learned to play the harmonica. One brother played any instrument that was put in his hands and another brother played the organ. Father played the drums because that was just keeping time and he could do it in any language.

When Jake was in the 3rd grade, before school each day, he ran his trapline; return home to bathe and change clothes before walking 1½ miles to catch the school bus. "Kids liked to be with me because I always made them laugh a lot. But a kid called me a dirty Russian and he got a black eye." Korell grew up with a lot of fights behind him averaging about five a day. The school's Professor Irwin and Jake saw a lot of each other. And that's when he got a whooping. The town kids thought they were better than the Korell's and would tease Jake and his siblings. Professor Irwin asked Jake when he was going to quit fighting and Jake told him when the kids stop calling him names. That's when he would quit fighting. He learned how to fight very well, eventually fighting professionally.

Jake's trick to trapping raccoons is to use a scent that they like – any fruit or vegetable smell – they like gardens. They also raid chickens so you can use the entrails of a chicken either fresh or let it rot. Use a little bit of fish scent on a piece of hide or dried cow platter pour a little bit on it and set the trap back about ten inches and you will catch a raccoon every time he walks by. As a kid Jake sold the raccoon hides for $2 to $3—they aren't worth much more than that today.

The trouble began when Jake trapped skunks. The schoolroom turned warm and Jake smelled terrible -- teachers regularly ran him home between the English and German school. When one of the teachers asked Korell why I didn't quit the skunks until I got an education; Jake told her that he liked skunks better than teachers. Jake would not be able to attend school for about six months of the school year for he had to help harvest in the fall and sow the field in the spring. He finally made it through the 6th grade when they kinda like expelled me from school for stinking, fighting and telling

dirty stories. For a while the German Lutheran pastor taught him, in German, of course. Jake was confirmed in German when he was fourteen.

Martha and Jake about 1938

Jake would find a skunk's den and stake an eight foot long piece of barbed wire in front of his den where he goes back and forth and then put the #1 Victor trap (which was easy for kids to use) in his den. Since he was trapping them out of their dens he didn't generally use any bait. But if he was trapping elsewhere he would use an old rotten sucker or carp for bait. Jake would let the fish rot all summer and then in the fall (about the 1st of October when the skunks were prime) and after the beet harvest was over, Jake would start trapping skunks with double sets in a row.

With a rotten fish there were sometimes two or three of them trapped at the same time. Every time he caught a skunk Jake would pull the peg and drag the varmint quite a ways from the den. He lead

Jake and his antique 50 caliber Hawken gun. Hawken was the mountain man's weapon of choice. It was specially built for use in the West.

them away real slow or else they would throw scent. If they threw their scent it would be a warning to the other skunks and they would leave. Also if the skunk died in the den where the trap was there would be a smell that would be a warning of danger to the other skunks. If the young trapper made quick moves or got too close the skunk would spray Jake. After he killed the skunk he would reset the trap. He caught as many as eleven skunks out of one den. Just one right after the other for Korell never caught less than three or four in a den site.

Jake sent his pelts to Stephen's in Colorado or F. C. Taylor in St Louis. Later he would send them to Sears because Sears paid more. He

would wrap good, dry skunk pelts in a gunny sack and sew them up with a potato sack needle before putting them in a couple layers of brown paper so they wouldn't smell so bad. He was paid $2.50 to $4.00 per skunk pelt depending on the stripe, some had short stripes, some had long stripes, some were wide and others narrow. The price increased with the amount of black color on the pelt. In about a week there would be a nice check in the mail. Soon afterwards other trappers asked if they could ship their furs with his, and Jake's business blossomed.

At the age of 11, Jake was trapping skunks, ermine, badgers, mink and muskrats. Within another year he was also trapping beaver, bobcats, and raccoon along the cedar breaks of the North Platte River between Lingle and Fort Laramie.

In the winter months when the morning chores were done he rode and walked trapping 260 skunks plus a lot of other animals in one

Jake and Martha Korell building their adobe house in 1938 near Kinnear with 1928 Chevrolet in background.

year. He broke work horses and a few saddle horses. He trapped quite a lot on horse back. Korell used to ride to old Fort Laramie and dig bullets out of the old thick sod walls. Fort Laramie was at the crossroads of a nation moving west. French-Canadian beaver hunters were the first men of European origin to explore the headwaters of the North Platte. The fort is named for one of these early Canadian trappers, Jacques La Raimee. Most of Jake's mentors were trained by these mountain men. Jake still uses these techniques, and other times he has figured out other ways work better. There was a grave on their farm where thirty soldiers were buried. One was officer, Grattan. All the men were killed by Indians in 1854. In the summer Jake would cut the long prairie grass into winter feed for the horses around the grave of the soldiers killed in the massacre.

At the age of 13 Jake went to work as a farm and ranch hand. He continued to trap in the winter months as well as feed cattle and did other ranch jobs. His family followed the old custom that everything went to the oldest boy, they took his trapping money and there were no prospects of him ever inheriting anything. So Jake left home when he was 16 years old. He had trouble with his older brother and father. One would tell him what to do and the other would tell him something else to do. The brother was mean to Jake, often hitting him on the side of the head. Jake took it for as long as he could and then told his father that he couldn't work for two bosses. Jake stayed with his

Uncle Jake and helped pick corn and make moonshine whiskey.

The Great Depression meant hard times for 13 to 15 million people who were out of work for 25% of America's work force had no way to support their family. Farmers and ranchers experienced the worst of the hard times getting as little as two cents a pound for hogs and butter and meat cost thirty cents a pound. In 1932 Jake worked for farmers and ranchers in the summer but starting about the middle of October he trapped until spring. His trapping and hunting has continued to be a major part of his income and kept the wolf from the door.

Jake's children and wife; Jerry, Lee, Jane and Martha Korell (1949). Their friend, Lew Diehl recently wrote, "Jake married well – Martha has been a hard working partner and mother to their children and granddaughter. This would certainly be a wonderful world should we all be as considerate and thoughtful of others as this down to earth family."

Jake's confirmation picture –
he's standing 2nd from the right

While working for one of the of the ranchers near the Nebraska border Korell looked at Martha Gradwohl who lived in the neighboring state and never stopped looking. Her parents didn't like him much so they eloped to Torrington, Wyoming, and were married on March 9, 1936 in the German Lutheran Church.

In December of 1936, Jake and Martha visited her folks in Riverton, Wyoming, for the holidays. The couple decided Riverton would be a good place to live for the area is surrounded by the Owl Creek and Wind River Mountain Ranges which would offer Jake plenty of places to trap.

For the first year Jake and Martha worked for Jake Haun, Sr.'s sugar beet farm. Jake would wake up at 3:30 a.m. to run the traps. By the time the other farmers were waking up Jake often had 30 to 40 muskrats skinned and stretched. In

the next year they purchased a 240-acre homestead for the past due taxes. They broke it out of sagebrush, seeded it to alfalfa and grass and built an adobe house. They raised cattle, sheep and horses and trapped in the winter months. Coyotes were wreaking havoc on the young couple's sheep herd, so Jake got some greyhounds and hunted coyotes with the dogs during the summer months.

Outfitting and Guiding

In 1940, Jake and Martha went into the outfitting business to supplement their ranching and trapping income. During WWII Jake did not serve in the army, as he was too valuable with what he did with his farm and providing coyote's pelts to be used for the hoods of uniform parkas.[1] Jake and Martha owned and operated an outfitting business for 26 years. Martha spent each fall in the hunting camp, cooking the best food you ever tasted, chopping wood for her cook stove, carrying countless buckets of water from the creek and charming clients with her beautiful smile and gracious manner. Jake guided and entertained hunters with his colorful tales and jokes, always wearing a big grin and his eyes a- twinkling. Lasting friendships were formed between Jake and Martha.

---

[1] After 1936 Jake and Martha lived in Fremont County, Wyoming (unless stated that it was some place else) all stories happened there.

Jake

No one was at the camp during a very heavy snowstorm. The old group of hunters had left and the new ones had not yet arrived. When Jake and Martha finally got through the snow drifted road, there was only the cook tent standing. The sleeping tents had ripped down from the weight of the snow. As they entered the cook tent to try to pop some snow off, the tent ripped and collapsed. Without a useable camp, they packed up and moved out. Everything was about to be packed out except a two horse trailer. The little Willy's Jeep couldn't move it in that much snow. Jake's grand mare, Toots, was

hooked to the trailer and was able to pull it out. The hunter's deposit had to be returned due to no camp left from which to hunt.

Jake and Martha always loved horses and taught their children to ride. Jake was a cunning horse trader and salty bronc rider, and don't sell Martha short on horsemanship. During one of their hunting camp expeditions, a nasty palomino, Yellow Cake, bucked the pack off three times in twenty minutes. That was all Jake could stand. The horse was no good for packing so Martha had to switch horses. And Martha rode Yellow Cake, and my golly she did.

Jake walking on his hands.

Jake went to Dubois, Wyoming to learn the art of taxidermy from J. Bob White. He then set up his own taxidermy business to go along with the outfitting business.

Civet Hat

Jake shakes his head and pulls his whiskers before he starts, "I was skinning out a little civet cat (spotted skunk) that I'd trapped when I accidentally punctured the scent pouch, getting the smelly stuff not only on my clothes, even my whiskers as well. Had to throw the clothes I was wearing away and washed well" He shakes his head before he continues, "I really scrubbed my beard, and even used tomato juice, but nothing worked. The smell was just too much for my good wife, Martha, and I had to sleep alone a couple of nights. No amount of begging and pleading would allow me back into the bedroom. Finally, in desperation, I had to shave off my beard. Didn't really want to do it for I had grown my beard for a good number of years. It worked, and I was, once again, allowed into the house. I tanned the civet cat and made it into a hat which I still wear."

Muskrat hide on stretcher. Note that the fur side is in and the skin side out. Prime hides need to be all pink. If there is black on the hide it isn't prime. Stretching the hide in this manner allows the fur buyer to know if your pelts are prime and will allow you the best price.

Jake will reveal some of his secrets of trapping success in this book. As you read Jake's wisdom and experiences in Wyoming, please check with the regulations in the area you plan to hunt or trap. Laws differ from place to place. Anyone who is interested in becoming a better trapper will gain valuable insights with his proven methodology that is within the pages of this book.

Chapter Three – Wolf, Fox and Coyote Tales

The night is darkening and the stars are blinking in a coal sky. There is no man made sound in this high country but far off in the hills the coyotes are calling their lonesome haunting tones and replying.

Current Predator Problems

"Do we still need predator control?" the dude asked as the fire's embers glowed in the dark.

Jake pulled his beard for a long moment before answering that when as many as 60 million buffalo trampled in the plains turning the prairies into seas of black nature took care of it. But in one year Buffalo Bill Cody alone killed 4,280 for the Union Pacific Railroad. By the mid 1880's the herds were virtually wiped out by hunters and climatic changes. Now the wolves and coyotes that had followed the herds culling out the old, young or injured animals for their meals turned to the cattle and sheep herds of the settlers. In the Dunoir Valley alone the Washakie pack of reintroduced wolves not only kill the ranches' stock and dogs; but friends of mine watched a herd of 1500 elk this spring being worried by the Washakie band of wolves. Six months later the wolves had killed

Glassing for Coyotes

Jake with a silky white coyote pelt

every calf. How can the elk continue that way? Jake feels that the predators need to be controlled but not wiped out. He enjoys seeing the wildlife as well as anyone, but if the predators are not controlled there could be no sheep or cattle raised in Wyoming. None of us wants to make an animal extinct.

The Coyote that Almost Won

The life of a trapper is not an easy one, and Jake has had some close calls. A coyote trap, anchored with a 20-inch stake, had been pulled up and drug away. Jake began trailing the big coyote and followed him four miles from Muddy Ridge to Teapot, and the tracks finally ending at a six-foot gully that came to a point. Jake circled the area and discovered the big coyote hiding in Russian thistle at the point of the wash. Not having a gun, he decided to try to knock the animal out by kicking it. He braced his hands on the rocks in the narrow wedge, swung his foot and slipped. The big coyote sunk its teeth into the calf of Korell's right leg, and he fell on top of the animal.

His leg clamped between the coyote's jaws, Jake was forced to choke it to death before it released his leg. When he got home and his wife got a good look at his leg, Martha insisted that he see a doctor to at least get a tetanus shot. However Jake did not want any part of that ordeal, replied, "The only shot I need is a shot of Red Eye scotch." The scotch worked because the leg healed on its own.

Easy Trapping & Hunting

Jake feels that trapping was easier when he was younger. The country was freer then than it is now. There wasn't the competition and the animals like the coyote could be called in. But you had to do it right because a coyote is smart and very often can't be called in a second time. Even after he was married and trapping west of Riverton, Wyoming, he recalls, "I used to be able to ride from around Pavillion to where Boysen Lake is and not see anybody all day. I had a Model A Ford without license or lights or brakes and the coyotes were gentle then – there weren't as many people shooting at them. It wasn't unusual to see a dozen standing around. I could get the Model A on one of those sheep wagon roads and curve toward 'em – and I'd get up pretty close and they wouldn't even notice until I threw the door open and the greyhounds would jump out. That's when the fun begins."

Jake and Kese

Cunning Coyotes

The coyote is by far the smartest animal in the whole world. He knows of people who tried all their life to catch a coyote and never caught one. Korell determines how many coyotes are in an area and if it is worth trapping by his experience. Any low place on a ridge and a trail going through is generally a good location. Jake also looks for sign in the sand, snow or dirt. If there is a lot of sign in the area Jake generally makes group sets. He makes four sets then moves half a mile or more in another area in the same valley and makes another group of sets. Jake likes to cluster trap. Sometimes he makes doubles so that he gets a pair or more.

Jake has seen coyotes come into his sets for a hundred yards. With their tracks in the snow Jake could see where the coyote picked up the scent walked right over to my set and were caught in the trap. When Jake started trapping coyotes in the '20's their hides were worth $8.00 apiece. He feels that coyotes are the most difficult animals to trap. He advises that in the fall you check over your traps to be sure the trigger and pan work freely. Boil the traps in plain water for about twenty minutes to remove all the junk from last year and then pour the water off and rinse the traps in hot water. Never wash the traps in detergent as it leaves a smell the coyotes can detect. Any scum which forms on the top of the solution when simmering should be skimmed off.

One month's cache

Dry them on a clean piece of cardboard or plywood. Next you need to dye and wax the traps. Make sure you are wearing rubber trapper's gloves every time you handle them with your hands. Clean rubber gloves work best for this and can be easy to clean even in a brook or in snow when you are in the field. When you are ready to take your traps out in the field put some dirt in a bottom of a clean box and put a couple of dozen in each box. When you have set a box full go back and put more traps in the box.

"Since coyotes are by far the most cunning animals I trap," Jake observes. "You have to take extra precautions like dying your traps and making sure you are extra clean when you set them or you just won't get any. You need to have clean gloves and kneel on a pad when setting a trap. Quickly set a long spring number three trap or a number two coil spring. They both work well. I like a flat set here something is propped up so they can only come in one way. Set the trap back about twelve inches and three to four inches to one side of the scent post and a white bleached bone that also attracts the coyote that is propped up against a sagebrush or rock and pour about a tablespoon of the scent I make out of rotten mare afterbirth. It works really well for coyotes. Do not set traps directly in a trail where any

passing animal can be caught but set them a little off the trail where the coyote has to go to check out the scent lure." Jake uses his rotten mare afterbirth lure but for coyotes he adds musk and asfetidia. At the time of publication Jake sells this coyote bait at $50.00 per gallon plus shipping.

Kese

Sometimes Jake goes to places he has trapped before, and other times ranchers call Korell because they are having a problem with the coyotes. For instance, in August of 2003 a couple of sheep ranchers asked Korell to do predator control for their flock. The young pups are taught (by their mother) how to hunt the lambs. But the young coyotes don't have the technique down and leave wounded lambs to suffer and die from their learning game. Jake's dog has taught himself how to be a partner in this chore. The Australian Red Merle Shepherd,

Jake's trapper tool

Kese, will go off about 100 feet and sit down. From behind a bush Jake calls the coyotes first with a howl and then they answer. This gives Jake an idea of where they are. His next step is to work closer to where they howled and start to use a distressed rabbit call. The coyotes think they are going to get a free meal. The coyotes fix on the dog and come after him. Kese will start growling as the coyotes get near which keeps them from either looking for Jake or bolting. As the coyotes get closer Jake has a chance to make doubles. A lot of time if a pair is coming Jake gets them both. This is simply predator control; their pelts aren't any good at this time of year.

Jake and Kese

New Way to Start Cold Jeep

When it was 10 – 12 degrees below zero Jake was out running his trap line with two of his hounds. He didn't get back to his civilian Jeep until almost dark. The oil had gotten really stiff and Jake had run the battery down trying to start the Jeep. He was up on Beaver Rim and he would have had to walk fifteen miles to the closest ranch. While Jake was sitting there wondering what he should do, he had a bright idea. He gathered sagebrush and warmed the oil. He jacked the hind wheel up and put it in high gear and pulled on the wheel. That turned the motor over and it started. He pushed it off the jack and got home about eleven that night. The family was worried, but Jake told them not to ever worry about him. He had coffee and sandwiches and he could have crawled into the little cage where the dogs are kept warm if he had to. He would have made it all right either way.

Oza Dollars & Sense

In 2001 Jake was hired by The Joe Oza Sheep Company of Arizona, to catch the sheep killing coyotes. In a ten month period Jake killed 364 coyotes in the vicinity of the herd. During the prime season Jake also caught bobcats, raccoon and badger. The previous year saw a 400 plus lamb kill by the coyotes, the year Jake worked the herd the lamb loss was less than 20. A $20,000 loss versus a $1,000 loss. Korell says that coyotes almost always kill lambs as long as they are available. After the lambs are shipped the coyotes will target young, fat ewes to kill, very seldom will they kill old sheep.

Jake believes that there will be two things left in this old world if warring factions try to wipe us out – Crooked politicians and coyotes.

Old Wolver

As a youngster Jake knew Tom Carr, an old wolver, when there was a $50 bounty on wolf pelts. He belonged to a family that helped eradicate the wolves that were down here in Wyoming and the edge of Nebraska. Tom was the youngest one and he was the only one alive when Jake was a little boy. Carr told Jake lots of wolf stories about the wolves coming in and killing their horses.

The wolves would run around the herd. The stallions and mares would stay on the outside and the yearlings and two year olds would stay in the center of the circle. When one of the wolves would be hit by the hooves of a stallion he would take quite a tumble. So the wolves kept circling until one of the young horses was near the out side of the circle. Then the wolves would grab him and start biting his legs until he was hamstrung and couldn't stand. Then they would eat him and the herd would scatter.

Carr also told Jake how he and his brothers snuck up and killed some of them with 30-30's. Wolves can go fifty to a hundred miles a day, but they always make sure there are gullies and washouts to hide in flat county. In the timber they always had plenty of protection. He trapped most of the state and noted that the wolves were being driven up to Yellowstone with people settling and hunting pressure. The first wolf spotted in Yellowstone was in 1922—about the time Jake saw Carr kill his last wolf. Carr feels that the wolves were never part of the original Yellowstone ecosystem. The reason to get rid of the wolves was that when there were no more buffalo they started killing all the game and domestic animals. Really slaughtering them. That reason is still there today with the new wolves they put in. They're doing the same thing.

Customer Satisfaction

Jake has been a successful master trapper for eighty-four years. Jake likes to foot trap because if he finds out that the caught animal is not the one that is the predator he was hoping for he can let it go. One of his North Dakota customers for his coyote scent says Jake's scent is better than most he uses. One day the customer trapped a wolf. Wolves were illegal to kill at that time. So the customer got the game warden who tranquillized the animal and tagged it before releasing it. The game warden now uses Jake's scents for the predator work he does.

Jake's Favorite Trap Sets

Flat set

While Jake knows lots of different ways to set a trap he has four favorite ones that he uses the most; mouse hole, bone set, auger and flag. They are all walk through type of sets.

He catches more with flat sets than any of them. (In about the center of the picture – lower left you will see some wool that Jake has poured some of his coyote scent on.) By the time he works the scent you got him.

Jake likes to vary his trap sets partly because the coyotes get wise to one kind of set. (He also changes his scent lure for the same reason.) He says that a lot of times he will use a piece of wool up on the sagebrush to act as a flag attractor. He will pour his scent on it. It is a variation of the set, when they get used to one kind he will switch around. Place a piece of paper under the jaws so it doesn't have to lift the paper with the dirt. This also makes sure that there isn't dirt under the pan that will block it from springing. The flag can be any kind of piece of hide, but you can't use game animals, it has to be from a domestic animal like cow, sheep, or game chicken.

Jake never kneels because if you kneel you leave scent. A lot of guys can't work like Jake does; but he says 'if you gotta kneel you better kneel on a piece of canvas or hide so the coyote can't smell that. Because when you kneel that stays there for a week.' Place the trap level with the ground and then put a piece of paper over the pan so that it leaves a hollow place so that it will spring when he steps on the pan.

Tag – you have to have your name or life time number which the game warden can check with the state and know whose trap it is.

The size of trap I use for bobcats, badgers and coyotes is mostly #2 coil spring. Sometimes Jake brushes the area with his trapping gloves. He pulls his hand back and if he springs the trap it just gets the fingers of his glove. He takes a piece of brush and wipes out his tracks when he backs away. That makes that set look natural just like the rest of the ground.

Make sure your trap is bedded good and solid. Always make sure that the trap is buried low enough so that it is level to the ground. Always make sure that the trap is bedded good enough so he steps on

the jaws and it don't wiggle. They will feel it when they walk and you will miss them or they will jerk back and you get a toe catch.

Another trap set is made by propping a bone next to a sagebrush. Jake puts some of his coyote scent in the cavity of the bone as a lure and props it up against a sagebrush or rock. This is a walk thru set, they will come through here. In clay soil Jake stakes the traps with a chain connected to a rebar rod. In sandy soil Korell uses a drag or cross stakes.

Then with a metal sifter put a light layer of dirt, about a quarter of

inch deep, until it is level with the rest of the ground and take some leaves off a sagebrush and scatter those over the top to make it look real natural and you don't know that the trap is there. The reason for using the sifter is that it keeps the rocks and sticks out of your set and to make it look like the rest of the ground. Try to get the trap at least 3" away off the side of the bone that attracts him. If you put it directly in line with the attractor they will have a foot on each side and you will miss them.

Level it – really smooth, sage brush sweep and then a few leaves and it looks natural. It looks like the rest of the ground and he doesn't know the traps there. When he comes into the smell he can only come in from one way to smell on that bone. The coyote then will walk up there and work the bone scent. Coyotes are five times smarter today than they were years ago. There's a lot more pressure on them today. Years ago we didn't have to boil our traps. You can use the set on fox, coyote, badger, or bobcat.

For the auger set, drill a hole the same way a small animal might dig a burrow. Place some sheep wool or dead mouse down the hole and put a little bit of grass at the mouth of the hole.

A dirt hole set is the same thing – you dig a hole on an angle. Pile the dirt up like a prairie dog hole. Just like an animal. Take a little piece of wool with scent on it and push it into the hole. Then he generally

takes a little bit of grass to kind of close the hole. Pretty soon they try to dig that up and by the time they're trying to dig it up you got 'em.

For the mouse hole set, go near a bush or rock on a bank dig a hole on a forty five degree angle and twelve inches deep with an auger. Put some scent down in the hole on something dry that will hold the scent like a cow pie or piece of wood. A lot of times Jake will put a dead mouse and scent down there for them smart old coyotes. Plug the hole with some real coarse grass. By the time the coyote has the plug worked out he is trapped. Sometimes you catch foxes, raccoon, badgers or bobcats. A lot of times Jake will put a dead mouse

and scent down there for them smart old coyotes. It looks like some kind of rodent dug a hole down there.

When making the set you have put it a little closer to the scent because the foxes and raccoons are a smaller animals. Put in sticks that any animal won't step on to direct him towards the trap. Gets some of your old smart coyotes that want to peek in there. It looks like some kind of rodent dug a hole down there. Again Jake put in a little grass plug and push it down.

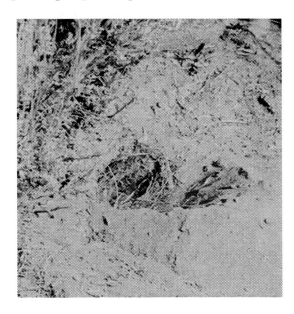

To catch a wolf, you use a trap big enough to hold him, which is double the size of a coyote trap. And you trap them exactly like you would a coyote. But you have to set the trap back about fourteen inches because he is a bigger animal and this will be where his front feet are planted. If the trap is too close to the bait or scent you are using he will just sniff around and leave.

Put the dog towards the scent post. If the set is the other way around when the coyote steps on the dog that can throw his foot out of the trap as it springs. You can push the springs back towards the dog until the jaws sets level with the pan. If the pan is set too high it leaves a bump on the ground that the coyote won't step on.

Train Tracks Thief

Jake was trapping foxes just south of Riverton when he kept missing the fox out of his traps. Finally he saw tracks coming from the railroad and Jake didn't see any car tracks. Korell couldn't figure why the train would take his fox out of the trap and then go back to the railroad tracks in the snow. He had heard of trains being robbed but Jake never heard of trains robbing people. Anyway one day he caught him. It was a train company's orange pick up made to ride the tracks. In the snow the wheels left a perfect impression of the track. The driver had just killed Jake's fox when Korell snuck up on him. Jake aimed for his jaw and he ducked down and he hit him on the forehead and broke Jake's hand. But Korell had knocked him down. Jake started kicking him until he was abeggin' and he left. Korell had no more trouble with him. He got back to Fuechsel's cabin and told him the story. He was living there by himself. He put some liniment on my hand. This story was written up by a local writer under the title of Don't Fence Me In.

Race with Coyote

In the '50's Jake was living out between Pavillion and Kinnear he had a couple of greyhounds and a big long trapline from the Barquin's coal mine to where Boysen Lake is now. Of course, Boysen Lake was only a river then, they hadn't put in the dam. In the winter back then Jake generally caught about fifty coyotes with the dogs and that many or more with traps. He would also catch other animals, too—like cats and raccoon. But the 'coons didn't start showing up until the '60's. Now we got so many that people along the river can't even raise a garden now. The raccoons even come to town and ruin people's gardens.

· Jake and Bobby Brown were hunting on John Osborne's ranch on Beaver Creek just south of the Bringolf ranch. They were unlocking a gate and there was a coyote standing there. That was another time Jake had forgotten his shells and there was only one shell in the 22 rifle. The coyote run off and Jake noticed he was limping a little but he was too far off to shoot by the time Korell got his gun. So Jake told Bobby to go up and run around the end of him and Korell would go down to the draw and when he came back by he'd shoot him. Bobby ran and then he started walking and Jake thought he better take over. So Jake ran over to where Bobby was. And he was half of Jake's age—and Jake was in his 60's. So Jake gave Bobby the gun and told him to go down by the creek. Bobby thought that the coyote was too far ahead. Jake took of running and ran and got ahead of him in the bottom of the draw. The coyote turned around and ran down the draw and he was only about 15 feet from Bobby. Bobby got him. Jake figured he'd run about 1 ½ miles.

Chapter Four – Horses and Wrecks

The horses are grazing quietly on the cool prairie grass. One or two had been hobbled and the rest were sticking close by. They seem to be attracted to the campfire and they often looked towards it. The moon has not risen and with no city lights the night sky looks like diamonds on a jeweler's cloth.

Korell Horses

Jake has always liked horses, and was the only one of the boys that could break them. Jake started using tractors instead of horses in their farming operation in 1945. At first they kept a couple dozen of them for their outfitting and hunting. Jake would check his traps on horse back. The 1950's were good years for farming. Jake always fed cattle and after the chores would run his trap line when he was still farming. He paid cash for a new 2-ton Chevrolet truck and new car and had money left. That would be very hard to do today. And that was back when a dollar was a dollar, not like it is today. Crop prices were bringing more than they are today. The Korell's were paid $1.05/lb. for wool, $50.00 each for lambs. Jake

fed cattle, in the winter he trapped and ran dogs on cats. In fact even today both Jake and his son Jerry still keep horses. In the spring of 2005 Jake was delighted that they had a new all black filly out of his son's stallion, Smoke N Sparks. With the raise in gas prices Jake is considering keeping his 4-wheeler in the barn this fall and again running his traps on horseback.

Bucking Mare

In the early '50's when Jake was young and strong and could ride anything that had hair on it, he had a neighbor that sold a horse to a doctor. The mare was broke pretty good. Pretty soon that mare started bucking the doctor off. So the neighbor brought the mare back. The neighbor tried to ride the mare but it bucked her off. So she got Jake try to ride it. Jake went over to their place and unloaded his saddle and went over to the round corral that the mare was in. Jake got her saddled and she humped up a little. She did a few jumps, but Jake rode her around the corral awhile. Korell told Don Murphy, the neighbor's father, to open the gate to let him out and take the mare down the road. The minute she got through the gate she started humping. She was agoin' high. Jake's car was setting there. She was bucking so high and taking such long high dives that the mare jumped over the hood of the car and never touched it while Jake was riding her. She landed on the other side. Jake had a chain quirt and put spurs on he started feeding the spurs to her and whipping. She started galloping. They galloped up the main road in front of the house for about half a mile. She was getting tired, but Jake made her run some more. She never bucked with Jake on again. He gave the neighbor back the horse after he couldn't get the mare to buck any more. The doctor got along with that horse for a month. But the mare must have known the doctor was afraid of her because she started dumping him again. The neighbor finally gave the doctor the money back and sold the horse to a cowboy family and they didn't care if she bucked a little. They got along great with her. They kept her.

Wagon Wreck

Jake remembers, "On my 10th birthday my older brother and I were hauling firewood from the river with a team of four horses. We went to cut some trees down and then whatever driftwood we could find. Finally, we had a big load of wood on a heavy beet wagon and left the wooded area to cross a stream of water with a steep bank when the wagon dropped off of the steep bank.

Jake was sitting backwards and hanging on while his brother was on the seat of the wagon. When the wagon hit the bottom it gave a big jerk.

Korell flew out of there backwards and grabbed for whatever he could get a hold of while he was falling. He got one hand on the single tree one hand on the horse's tail.

His legs were spread on each side of a front wheel so if that big load of wood would have gone over him, he would have been dead.

'My brother was white as a sheet when he looked down. I crawled out from under there and was okay. I wasn't hurt at all.'

Car Wreck

Wyoming's highway system is rooted in the days of the Old West. Pioneer trails between the East and West Coasts crisscrossed Wyoming and were the main routes across the Northern Rocky Mountains to destinations such as California and Oregon. With the development of the automobile, Wyoming's landscape changed dramatically. The roads in this era were dirt or gravel. Gasoline and oil became permanent fixtures, and long dirt stretches slowly evolved into long asphalt and concrete stretches. Wyoming began to oil several roads in the southeast corner of the state. This program was completed in 1929 with the oiling of 87 miles of roads. The state of Wyoming finished oiling the major roads in Wyoming by 1939. This marked the end of the remoteness and lengthy delay in transportation that had plagued the state since its territorial days. One of the major roads that got paved ran through Lingle, the old Oregon Trail. And this brought cars into Jake's life.

Jake's father's hired hand was a man by the name of Roy Hyer. He taught Jake how to make coyote bait and scent that he still uses today.

Roy worked all summer for Jake's father and said he could make more money working over at the beet dump where the sugar beets were delivered as a tare man. He would scrape the dirt off the beets and then weighed it and mark the tare down on the beets. (This amount would be subtracted from the amount the beets weighed when they first arrived at the beet dump.)

One evening Roy came to pick Jake up and they were going to go to a picture show. Jake knew he had been drinking, but didn't realize he was drunk. The road turned at the bridge. It was angled a little bit but Roy drove straight and went through the railing of the bridge. The car fell down in the water and the railing came through the radiator and the motor. It bent the dashboard and shot through the window. It tore off part of Jake's left eyebrow. He had a big gash that really bled. It even tore a big hole in Jake's new suit.

When the car hit the water there was one wheel sticking up in the back. Korell rolled the window down, and was about half dizzy. Jake's leg was ahurtin' and he had a black eye.

And it dawned on Korell 'where's Roy'. So he reached down and got him by the collar and got him up and he was still out. And Jake held him up.

Pretty soon Roy started spitting out water and coughing and said, 'I sure didn't have any luck today. I got pinched in town for driving drunk and now I've lost my automobile.' He sat there and looked around a little and then said, 'Lets get the hell out of here.' They swam to shore then walked home about five miles. Jake's boot was full of blood.

The next day Jake was driving four horses with a big load of beets and there was the newspaper guys taking pictures of that car down in the river. And they asked Jake if he knew anything about who owned this car.

'Ya, I was in it.'

And they thought he was lying to them. Korell showed them his eye. His eyebrow had been pasted back and he was limping.

Well, then they said 'who's the owner'.

Jake replied, 'He works over there at the beet dump. His name is Roy Hyer and he's taking tare over there.

When Jake got over to the dump he saw Roy pointing at me. He was telling the reporters that Korell was the one that was in the wreck. That story was in the newspaper. Roy bought a different car and just left the wreck lay there. It was all tore up.

Earning 1st Horse

"When I was about 12 years old John Burns had a string of cattle on our summer range across from Old Fort Laramie. We rode up there and there was a really nice sorrel stallion there. Boy was he a beauty! He had a little head and a nice pencil neck which I like. I don't like the big arched neck horses that don't rein good. He was just really the way I like 'em. So I said, 'John, I'd like to buy that two year old colt from you.'

John said that he would rope him and told me to get my saddle. "I will ear him down and if you can stay on him I will give him to you."

We snubbed him down and Old John Burns eared him down and I got my saddle on him.

John turned him loose and he bucked me off.

John said, 'Damn, I said stay on him. I'll give you another chance.'

So boy, the next time I got on him I grabbed a hold of that horn and I got him rode.

John castrated him right there. After he healed up I finished breaking him. By the time he was a four year old he was a good using horse. I was the only one out of three brothers that could stay on a horse. So I broke most of the horses that were used on the John Burns ranch. 'I tell people I never got bucked off but I got off a few times when I wasn't ready.'

Moving Cattle

Two years later, on my 14th birthday, I was on a four year old, and had him going good when I was moving cattle by myself from the John Burns ranch to the east pasture along the Platte River which was towards Lingle. It was a big, fenced pasture, between 1,000 to 2,000 acres. As I was riding along, I loosened up, (I never had a tight/deep seat) and a jack rabbit jumped up from under him and he jumped to the side and threw a big buck into me and he got me off and landed on the cobblestones and broke all my ribs on the left side. They were kinda pressed over to my lung 'cause I was bleeding out of my mouth. So some of them were scratching my lungs. Every time I tried to get up and walk towards home I passed out. Finally, when they found me in the middle of the afternoon, (the horse came home in the morning) and they came looking for me and with the dry grass they had trouble finding me. They finally found me and hauled me to the Scottsbluff Hospital. I was down there a month before I was strong enough to come home. After I healed up I put the horse in a round corral and used spurs and a chain quirt. He turned out pretty good after that. He was one of our better horses after that.

Dobash

My father traded for a dark brown horse that weighed about 1100 pounds. We called the horse Dobash after the man who had owned him. My cousin and I were riding along and the horse kept wantin' to go to the barn. We wanted to ride on by.

He got mad and started abuckin' and he bucked me into a mud hole. There was about 8" of water on top of some real soft mud. He stepped on my jaw when he bucked by. I passed

out and my cousin later told me that he had to pull like hell to get me out. He drug me out and he said I sat up, but I didn't remember doing it.

My cousin led me up to the house which was about a couple hundred yards. They sat me down and were cleaning me up and it finally come back to me what happened.

My jaw was broke and it's still wider where it healed. And I had big bumps on my tongue for years and years --in fact you can still the scars on it from where I bit it.

After I healed up I really had it in for him and I finally saddled him up in the round coral and I got the quirt and the spurs and I worked him over. When he wanted to quit bucking I made him do it some more until I wore him down until he was lathering. He never bucked again after that, but he did do one ornery thing.

He was big enough that we could use him in a sulky rake. I was raking hay when he stampeded and run off. He ran across an irrigation ditch with water in it and I bounced

32

off the rake in front of the teeth and the teeth raked me into the ditch. Then the teeth went over the top of me. I just lay in the ditch.

Dobash tried to turn the corner. He crashed the rake into the gate and tore it all to hell. The harness was all torn up. He crashed through the gate and went into his stall.

My father had to go into town and buy a new $100 12' dump rake. That was back when men worked for $1/day –so it took a while to pay for. I got a good cussing, but I was just a kid and couldn't hold him when he stampeded. I worked him over good before he went to do more raking.

Good Guide

Jake and Martha were out on their own hunting elk after they had closed their hunting camp Martha was a good horsewoman and loved to ride. They were back in Beauty Park and it was just snowing and blowing. You couldn't see ten feet in front of you. They were in some really thick timber way down south of the highway.

They had ridden so far that Jake didn't know if the Dot and Dash Trail was east or west. Martha was on an old buckskin horse named Joker that was mountain wise. He was just a good old mountain horse. So Jake told Martha not to touch her reins or try to guide Joker.

Jake swore he was going the wrong direction as Joker took them through some brushy old timber. He just kept going east. He knew what he was doing and where he was going even though Jake had his doubts a lot of times. He got on the trail and he was running/walking going to beat hell.

Jake looked up and saw some familiar mountain peaks and realized Joker had gotten them on the Dot and Dash trail. They were only about four or five miles from camp when they hit the main trail.

Silver Thistle

"I roped a two year old stallion on Oil Mountain east of Sand Draw. There was a horse they called Silver Thistle. He got away and got into this Oil Mountain herd. He bred a lot of mares and they always called the Oil Mountain herd grays –and this was where the gray came from. Almost all of them were gray colts. Well, I got this dappled gray stallion home and in the corral. I tried snubbing him up to a center post so I could put a saddle on and play with him. I had a straw hat on and he grabbed the hat and a mouth full of hair that all come out. He chomped at me. And I finally got him snubbed up and got a curry comb and started currying him. He kinda acted like he liked it and he quit kicking and fighting. Then I got him a pan of oats. Boy he sniffed on that and started eating that. The next day he was following me around like a dog. I was real kind to him. I would brush him and play with him. He didn't buck when I saddled him up. Boy he made a mighty fine cow horse. After I got him broke I made him into a nice gelding. "

Jake with two others of his kind.
Can you find him?

Fishing Trip

Back when I was young and strong and hard as a rock; Harold Brasie and I used to hunt together. On this trip both and Harold and I had each brought our wives. We knew each other well. We'd start bugeling and the elk would answer. We'd split up and sneaked in, one from one side, one from another. Year after year we had worked it out that way and we all always got our elk. We'd bugle until we were back together. When you have a good hunting partner it is amazing what you can do that way without getting lost in the woods. We each had a saddle horse and a big pack horse that took in our tent, groceries and stuff. We had about 200 pounds on

him for our fishing trip to Moccasin Lake. We were fishing about half a mile from where the horses were and had finally caught enough fish and we saw bear tracks in the mud about the middle of the afternoon. We left Lost Lake where the brook trout all weighed about a pound and a half to two pounds. Boy they bit. They bit real good. We caught our limit. We walked about half a mile to our camp where we had tied our horses. But now they were all gone. I noticed more bear tracks in the mud along the spring where they had been tied. I figured out what happened. The horses all tore loose and took off and went to Moccasin Lake (eight miles away) where the truck was. I dog trotted to my truck. When I got there I found they had stopped at my truck and then went on down the trail trying to go home. I jumped in the truck and run down the switch backs clear over towards Dickinson Park before I found them. I got ahead of them and I flagged them down and I caught the main leader, a big bay mare rope horse, the best saddle horse of the bunch. The others all stopped and I caught the others. I had extra ropes and a bridle with me as they all had halters on and the torn ropes. I backed the truck into a bank and I jumped them into the back of the truck and hauled them back to Moccasin Lake. Then I tailed them together, and of course I had to ride bareback. I was mad at them and I really pounded them back and they were all lathered up when we got back to camp. I had only been gone in a little over 3 ½ hours when I returned to camp about 8:30 pm. They all were really surprised that I was back in that short a time when I told them how far I had to go after those horses. The next day we packed out of there.

Jake's son Jerry

Toots

"I had this big bay mare, Toots, that didn't look like she could run. When Jerry, my son, was about ten years old I was helping Jack Thompson build fence on a sheep ranch. Jerry snuck this mare out the pasture and I didn't even know she could run. I had done some roping off of her.

Jerry took her over to the fair grounds and they had horse races at the fair. She was kind of fat and built kinda like a work horse. There was a registered quarter horse named Black Jack that everyone was betting on. Jerry was to race against him.

The crowd yelled, 'Hey kid, what are you going to do with that plow horse?'

Abe Lund knew she had never been out of a starting gate and told Jerry to hang on and that he would make sure that she got out of the starting gate.

And you know what – when that gate opened she acted like a pro. She beat Black Jack out of the gate. And

she won that race. Now the crowd's tune changed now that she won.

Jerry came home with a $100 bill in his pocket.

After that every race I put her in she won – just one after another. I'd have bets and just enjoyed beating the hind end off those other guys. It was generally a lap and tap start. Some guy would holler "go" and boy she was just so fast. She had two lengths of lead right off at the start. Then she could run like hell and I would win every time with her.

When I put her in a race with the Indians they would ask which race is Toots in? Then they would take their horses out and put them in a different race. 'Cause they knew they was going to get beat. The Indians didn't like to see me down there with Toots.

She was also a hella of a rope horse. Boy, she was a good horse. We had some good colts out of her too. But they couldn't run like she could though. Pretty close, but Toots was just outstanding.

Sick Yak

When I was working on the Diamond G ranch near Dubois, they had a yak as a pet and he got really sick. He was drooling out of his nose and Percy Yarborough told me to get on a horse and get that yak in. I drove him and he wouldn't go so I roped him. And boy was I glad he was sick because he jerked me and my horse over. He jerked to one side and was dragging us. I cut the rope and got the horse up. I got all the cattle that were around him and drove all the cattle and the yak over to the corral. There was a guy by the name of Tom Johnson that was working there and we got him in the barn. Tom got a hold of a rope and got it around a post in the barn to hold the yak and we got him doctored with penicillin. Got the rope off him and kicked him out. He lived. But he was awful sick for a while. But I was glad he was sick because he would have killed me.

Back Hoe Blues

A few days later I was using an old back hoe that I bought and platting out that land we bought. We had thirty plots there and I had sold fourteen of them. I drilled two wells and on each well I connected eight of those plats. I piped for water from the well. I got $9500 an acre for it. And that put me on easy street. I was jumping up and down. I would dig six foot deep and lay a big water 8" line. And then they had pipe dope to smear on that pipe and then I would slip the fiberglass pipes together and there was acid in it that would seal it. I was galled from jumping that pipe up and down.

And that smear felt good on my hand and looked like Vaseline. So I put some of it on the crack in my butt where it was really hurting.

It was like I put turpentine on it!

It started a burning!!

I jumped in the pickup and was taking my clothes off while I was driving to the canal. There was a guy that lived right there and he came over and said, 'boy when you decide to go swimming you really do it fast.'

And then when I told him what happened he was laughing so hard he was on his knees with tears in his eyes from laughing so hard.

I walked bow legged for several days before that quit hurting.

Polo Player

I was guiding up on the Diamond G and had this Englishman. He tried to hire me to go back to England with him. He wanted me to train horses for him. He had two daughters that I taught to catch trout and he thought that was the darndest thing. His name was Burton and he was a top polo player.

Bucking Horses

When the Diamond G bought the Brooks Lake Lodge from Foster Scott with 130 head of horses that they were only using about 30-35 of them. The rest were just running loose for years on the free range. Foster told Percy Yarborough that those horses have to be tried since they have been loose all these years. Some of them are kinda snorty. Some of them will even buck, so you have to try them and see which ones you want to keep. And which ones you are going to have to get rid of. It took me three days.

I roped every horse and worked all day long. I was raw. Thirty two of them didn't buck. I put them in a different corral. There was one they called Black Jack that bucked but not real hard. He had a real good running walk to him. He was kinda snakey but I kinda liked him. I put him in another corral and then there was King Arthur – I'll tell you about him in a minute. I liked him and he was tough. He also had a good running walk to him.

There was another one whose name was Ten Penny. He was ornery and would buck a little. And I put him in the same corral.

Then they had one they called Chicken that would buck a little that I also put in the same corral.

I told Percy that those buck a little but they would be good for the wranglers and cowboys that guided. But don't let the dudes around them. I told him the thirty two were good dude horses but the others he needed to can up because they were going to kill somebody. Some of the horses didn't get canned but ended up being rodeo bucking horses.

Percy and I bought about 100 head of good using horses to replace the ones we canned. The Diamond G was paying for them but they took me along to try them and I told them which ones were good and which ones weren't. If they were sound and gentle I told them to buy that one. So we got enough bought that they run the ranch in a big way.

King Arthur

I was riding a horse by the name of King Arthur—the one I told you I would tell you about. He was a big ornery horse over 1200 pounds. He would buck a little in the mornings but boy was he a traveling son of a gun. I liked to ride him. But you couldn't get off him. One time I found out what his bad trait was. I rode out to round up the dude horses for the Diamond G. I was working for them then. I got off for some reason and he would run by you and drag you and kick you and get away from you. And he was so stout that he could do it. Every time! And so I knew I couldn't get off of him.

Well, the cook over there fixed me a lunch and I had the wrapped sandwich in my shirt. When he heard me rattle that wax paper he threw a buck into me and I had a hell of a time getting that sandwich out and eaten.

And then I had to pee.

I didn't dare get off of him. So I hung it out and it dribbled down his shoulder and he felt that and he started abuckin'. That GD zipper just about sawed my penis off. I had a hell of a time.

When it finally quit hurting enough so I could handle it I put it away. I was sorer than hell for a long time.

Cutting Ice

In the 40's Jake and Martha did not have electricity or a refrigerator. So he took a wagon and team to Ocean Lake. Jake had an ice saw to cut out big blocks that weighed 100 pounds apiece. The lake would freeze solid from two feet to eighteen inches thick. He would take it home and put it underground in sawdust. Jake had made a little dug out with a roof for the ice house. He had hauled in sawdust from the sawmills. There would still be ice in there in the fall. That way they could make home made ice cream and refrigerate some of their stuff.

Wild Stud

There was a rancher by the name of Bill Mack who owned a bunch of land out by Pavillion. He took in 130 head of dude horses. He wintered them. The people lived high in the mountains and had to have a winter place for their horses. They trucked them clear over to Pavillion. Mack would keep them there until June when he was suppose to take them back. Mack was hired to drive them. It was cheaper than hauling the horses. They also hired Jake and Ed Harrington. Jake and Ed drove the horses. They left Pavillion and crossed the river up by Kinnear. Went up through Hudson and took the shortest route. They just cut across where there was no fences, just open range.

Jake had brought a bronc horse out of a wild herd. And that horse must have bucked fifteen to twenty times that day. He bucked until he was played out and Jake had to take another horse. They camped at the Sweetwater River just over South Pass. The horses were real tired by then. They were ready to rest the night.

Bill Mack followed with the sheep wagon and he'd cook for them. They just slept underneath it in sleeping bags.

During the night Korell heard some squealing and horse fighting going on. Jake woke Bill and told him. He said, 'It's too dark to do anything now. We'll just have to see in the morning what happened.'

In the morning there were seven of our pinto mares that always kinda hung together. Those seven mares were gone. We counted the rest of them and knew exactly what was gone. Just them seven was gone.

Just as Jake had suspected a wild stud had come in. He sorted them out and stole them. There was some horse tracks going west over the highway and there was horse tracks all over.

Bill drove the road with his pickup and Ed Harrington rode west.

They couldn't find anything. Jake saw there were some tracks on the other side of the highway going east. The tracks got fresher. Finally, Jake got down about four or five miles from the highway. Jake glassed the hillside and saw the mares down in a bunch of about 30 wild horses. There was a blue roan stud with a big mane and tail dragging the ground. Every time those mares tried to break away he lay his ear back and run around them and run them back into the herd.

Jake rode down about 50 yards from him and here he come. The wild stud come arunnin'. Jake could hear his teeth aclackin'. Snapping at me or my horse or something.

Jake could barely out run him even though he was mounted pretty good. Jake out ran the stud and got back to the sheep wagon. Jake grabbed an octagon barrel 30-30 rifle that had nine shells. He roped a thoroughbred lookin' horse. Korell knew that horse could out run the roan stud in case he got in trouble again.

Jake rode back there and here the ugly blue roan that had a big head came again. Korell knew the only choice he had to get the mares back.

Korell knelt down and had the reins wrapped around his arm. He waited until the stud got about 50 yards away and then he shot him right between the eyes.

Jake went over there and found that he never had a brand, he was a slick. He mouthed him and he was a six or seven year old. Range horses lose that cup that tells their age when they are nine. Then they call them a smooth mouth. This horse was just starting to lose his cup. Ranch horses start to cup out a year later than a wild horse. The wild horses graze more and get more dirt and they grind it off a little faster.

The mares cut out of the wild herd by themselves. When Ed and Bill showed up we joined them. We just kept them moving towards Pinedale where we were headed.

Jake's love for horses has not diminished through the years, and he still rides and goes on family annual hunting and fishing pack-trips.

Jake's daughter, Jane, rode before she could walk and went with the family on guiding trips. She hated it when she got old enough to go to school and had to stay home and take care of the stock and didn't get to go hunting. She competed in rodeos as a barrel racer. Jane was the Casper College Rodeo Queen and Wyoming Appaloosa Queen. When competing for the Appaloosa national title in Syracuse, New York, she had to use one of their horses as the distance was to far to take her own. The horse bucked when she got on him and the whole crowd yelled, "Ride 'em Wyoming" as she hung on and got him rode. The horse did well for her in the competition.

Jerry chariot racing

Kathy, daughter of Jerry and Iva, on Etcetera in 2003

Jerry's wife, Iva on Classy Barjo (above)

Jake's granddaughter, Kathy

Kathy with her parents Jerry and Iva Korell, (right)

DIAMOND CLASSIC FUTURITY TRIALS - DIVISION V

CENTRAL WYOMING FAIR	AUGUST 19, 1983	TRUCKLIN DANDY	GERALD KORELL	owner
HALF MOON KIRK	place	RACE 6	GERALD KORELL	trainer
TOUGHMOORE ESCOTT	show	350 yds 18.90	MIKE FLANAGAN	up

Barjo Twist won the 1st race at the Wyoming Fair in 1976 by running 350 yards in 18:64. There is a poem about him starting on page 90 of this book.

The Korell family always found a thrill in horse racing with many happy years at the track.

Chapter Five – Beavers

The full moon was high in the sky brightening the mountains to light and shadow. The camp fire feels good at this high altitude.

Jake traps beaver in the traditional way. His mentors were born during the mountain man era and were taught by them. For instance a beaver trapper, Old Man Wyldie, taught Jake along with his own two sons how to trap and skin beaver. During the noon hour Jake would grab his lunch and run over to the Wyldie's and watch him skin the beavers. He always came in about noon from the Platte River and Jake wanted to watch him skin them and they would visit while he worked.

Jake cooking beaver stew

Beaver Press

Korell took a picture of his beaver press with an old Brownie camera and took the measurements and now he has one sitting at home. It was used to press the beaver to bring them out of the mountains on horses and mules. The mountain men would take sixty plews and fold them hair in to protect the fur. They would put one hide down then the next one would be placed so the folds were turned and the pile would be flat. When they got sixty in a pile they would press the hides down and tie ropes around then. The pile was only about the size of a pannier that you use in the mountains with a horse. And they would have two bundles on each horse or mule.

The mountain man trapped a little different than what is done now. The mountain man would wade out into the river to where it was deep enough to drown a beaver and pound a dry pole or limb into the mud. They would have about a seven foot chain on the heavy trap they used back then. When the beaver got into the trap he would swim and get that long chain wrapped around the pole and drown. Another way used in a pond was to have a dry float stick and then the mountain man would have to look for the float stick to find the drown beaver. He would wade out there to pull the beaver in.

Jake holding a blanket beaver. Blanket size is a total of 66" when adding the diameter from nose to tail and then the perpendicular diameter.

Jake runs 120 mile trapline has more than 100 traps which he checks either daily or half of them one day and half the next. Jake feels that there is nothing more fun than getting out and running his own trapline, and because of his years of experience he is successful much more of the time than not.

Jake believes that the most difficult animals to skin are beavers and badgers because their hides are tight on the carcasses and you have to use a knife to cut the hide off the animals.

When he was young he was shown how to skin so he never ruined any furs. Beaver and muskrat are skinned about the same. "First cut off the feet so the hide will go through. Then start cutting down by his flat tail and go clear up to his chin and lips. And lay him wide open," Jake explained. "When I skin I go back quite a ways before leaving any of the back plate on because when you are fleshing if there is too

much meat on the hide that's where you will cut it first. Next take off the oil sack so you will have good clean castors. The oil sack is used for making lures. Then take off the pair of castors. I let them semi dry for a couple of days before I put them in the deep freeze. They sell better if they are partially dried."

Jake goes back to the hide before continuing. "Scrape all the flesh off the hide. He is a real humped back and when you stretch a beaver it comes out round. And that's the way the mountain men would do. They would take a set of willows and they would lay it down and peg it and bring into a round about the size of the beaver hide and rawhide it together. They would then lace the beaver skin on to the willow hoop with sinew or copper wire was sometimes used."

Korell first got $6.00 to $7.00 for beaver, later it got as much as $50.00 to $60.00, but now they bring about $20.00.

The Conibear trap consists of two metal rectangles hinged together midway on the long side to open and close like scissors and is intended to be an "instant killing" device. It is set in their paths where the animals

go up and down to feed. Or you set it in the front of their den, or where they are going into their lodge. Most of the river beaver are bank beaver and in ponds they live in lodges. You need to wade out into the pond and feel around with you feet to find where the den is going up into the lodge and you will catch him every time. You set a snare where they are going up and down the banks to chew on the trees. There is a place for all kinds of traps; foot traps, snares or Conibear's. It depends on the location where you want to set it.

The Burlington Northern Railroad called him to trap beaver that were causing flooding of railroad tracks north of Riverton. He has always been successful in eradicating the marauders.

Beaver and Muskrat Trap

Jake laid out a beaver set on dry land so pictures could be taken and an underwater camera was not available.

44

Put the trap in four to six inches of water. Take a stick above the trap set in about four inches of water and stick it into the mud and use some castorium (from the scent gland of the beaver) to attract the beaver.

Lock on trap set—the beaver swims as far as the lock slides down the wire when he tries to turn around it locks. The beaver is then stuck under the water.

Then use about a ten pound chunk of iron and put on about an eight foot piece of smooth slide wire with an L- shaped connection to the trap so when the beaver gets in the trap he follows the wire and when he tried to turn around it would lock and wouldn't let him get back and he would drown. A beaver (and muskrats) have to be drowned or in a few minutes, or they can wring their front (trapped) foot off and get away. The beaver caught in the trap will work until it's solid and then spin around until their foot is off

and there would be an escaped three legged beaver.

No matter what you are trapping be sure to stay clean. Use rubber foot wear and lined rubber gloves and keep them really clean. If you get either of these bloody or dirty you can easily clean them in the snow. And rubber doesn't leave any scent like cloth or leather if it is kept clean. Jake hangs all his trapping and hunting clothes in the garage so they don't pick up any cooking, etc smells in the house. He also doesn't let anyone who smokes or chews ride in his truck.

Chapter Six -- Elk Anecdotes

The campfire has burned down and the coals snap and glow brilliant orange as Jake starts another tale.

Martha's Elk

In the early '60's Jake and his wife were running a hunting camp. They had some hunters flying into Dubois. We had a little time so since Martha had an elk permit they decided to go hunting. Jake had one also, but he wanted to get hers out of the way first. They went about five miles away from camp. Jake spotted a cow elk on the hillside. Martha's first shot hit her but wasn't a killing shot. Jake went back to his saddle bag to get some more shells, but the wind had blown his saddle over in the night and they had been dumped out. There were no more shells. The elk couldn't go uphill and so was making her way down to a patch of timber. Since they didn't want to leave her there to suffer they came up with a plan. Martha would take a long pole and drive her out of the timber while Jake would ride around with an axe. The cow was standing there kind of sick and then she came galloping out. The stout horse Jake rode was a good bulldogging horse that weighed between twelve and thirteen hundred pounds. That good rodeo horse ran right alongside that elk just as he had been trained to do for the rodeo. Jake reached over and hit her between the ears with that little axe. She fell down in front of the horse. Jake hit the ground slid one way in the snow. The horse stumbled and lay on his side. The horse had fallen upside down and slid away from Jake. Korell went over and cut the elk's throat and dressed her out. Jake put the whole elk on the horse and made it back to camp by dark.

Corralling Elk

Another time Jake was guiding and running a hunting camp near

46

Togwotee Pass behind the Togwotee Lodge. Jake was riding towards Cub Creek, about four miles from the lodge there was a big meadow called the Rainbow Meadow. There was a bunch of elk just before you came to the meadow. The guy crawled off his horse and shot a nice bull. And the bull humped up and ran. There was an old corral alongside of the trail and the bull got in the corral. It was open on one side and he couldn't get out. He collapsed and died right there. Jake was dressing him out and another guide and some of his hunters were riding through and they asked why the elk was in the corral. Jake told them that they always corralled his elk before they shot them. The hunters knew Jake was lying and so they just laughed and rode on.

California Dreaming

In Vic's camp there was this California guy and one morning at the breakfast table there was this guy, his wife Ruth, me and another hunter. There was also a nurse that had a two weeks vacation that was helping as a cabin maid. The California guy was talking really filthy. And I said, 'hey, shut your God damn mouth. I tell some pretty rough stories around men, but I half way talk decent around women. Why don't you just shut your mouth?' Boy, he clamped up.

The next night Wayne, Neil, Jerry and this same guy from California were playing penny ante poker. I walked by, I had taken a guy out and he had killed a small moose and he didn't want to mount the head. He just chopped off the horns and the head was laying there. I cut an ear off it and put it in the Californian's sleeping bag. And then I went to bed.

When the guys quit playing poker we heard the damnedest racket in the next tent. He had tried crawling into his sleeping bag and felt the ear and the guy that was sleeping in the tent with him said he crawled out of his bag like an arrow out of bow. He took a flash light and looked in there and said, 'I bet I know the dirty bastard that done that –that old Jake. I got a bone to pick with him in the morning.'

The next morning about daybreak I was tying up three horses – one for me and two for the hunters I was suppose to take.

The California guy come out and said, 'I'm gonna whip your ass.' He was a lot bigger than me.

And I said, 'Well, I generally don't set my machine for such a small job, but I'll do it this morning.' I took my jacket off. Jake had had boxing lessons and had boxed professionally.

He took one look at me and I was all ready. He turned around and walked back into the tent and that was over with.

Clarence was watching around the corner and he started giggling and said, 'Guess you handled that about right.'

The next year the California guy called Clarence and said, 'I'd like to book an elk hunt with you.'

Clarence agreed.

The California guy asked if that Jake guy was going to be there.

Clarence told him that Jake was one of the best guides he ever saw.

The California guy replied that then he wasn't coming.

Clarence told him good, we don't need him that bad.

He didn't want to come around where Jake was, 'cause Jake probably would have gotten into it with him – and I was still in pretty good shape.

Broken Arm Shooter

One time one of the wranglers put one of the hunters on kind of a rank horse. Clarence didn't even know about it. The horse bucked him off and broke his arm. He had two days left in his hunt. My hunters had filled their licenses. I was just setting around resting. Clarence said that this hunter wanted me to take him out. I said that wasn't fair to me, because my two hunters had filled their licenses. It wasn't fair to ask me to help a guy get his elk when he only has one day left. But Clarence coaxed me into taking him out anyway agreeing that whatever happens happens. It snowed a little that night. We left early in the morning and we rode down out of Colburn Creek and then we circled back around just about straight south. There was a bench up there that was full of timber. I knew if there was any elk they would be up around there. We got around on that bench and saw elk tracks. So we tied up our horses and we walked up real slow to some big boulders there. There was a nice bull in the park there. I got his gun all ready since he had his arm in a sling. I said, 'lay your gun on the rock' and he shot and knocked him down. I dressed him out, quartered him and took him over to a big high cliff – and it was straight south and you either had to go way around or straight up the road under the cliff which was half the distance. I threw the elk off the cliff down to the bottom. We rode back with the horns on my horse. I hung them over the horn. I told Clarence what we had done. Clarence said he

would get up early in the morning and get the elk. We went up and got the meat. Then there was this big story in the newspaper about me taking this guy out with a broken arm and getting him up on the elk and how he shot this elk.

Lee's Elk

Jake's son, Lee got polio when he was 13 and rode a wheelchair for the rest of his life. When Lee was a teenager he would get a permit (from the game warden) to shoot from a pickup since he was a paraplegic. Up at the Diamond G Ranch the foreman told Jake and Lee that they could hunt up there. Jake and the foreman were the same age and had been through a little together up there on that ranch. They drove up to the timber and Jerry; Jake's 2nd son rode up through the timber. There were some elk standing up there and Jerry got in behind them and ran the elk past the pickup. Lee hung out of the window to get a bead. When he shot the 7mm mag it jumped back and the scope punched him above the eye. It caused a big sore. But Lee had nailed the elk. The same year he also got a four point buck deer and an antelope. Lee was a good shot. Jake had taken his sons out to prairie dog town and one would keep shooting until he missed and then the other one would shoot until he missed. Both of the kids got to be damn good shots. Jake taught his kids gun safety and neither the boys nor Jake ever had an accident with a gun.

Jerry's First Elk

Jerry turned 14 on the 4th of September which was the legal age to hunt. Jake and Jerry were walking along the ridge and they could smell elk. Sure enough they jumped a five point (western count) bull running straight down that ridge ahead of them. Jake raised his gun and got a bead on him. But Jerry shot first and he hit him. He knocked him down. So Jake didn't have to shoot. It was his first elk, and he was as proud of it as he could be. That was all he would talk about for a couple of days. Jake feels he was that way, too, when he shot his first elk.

Bull Mountain Hunting

In the '70's Jake was trapping on the Mayland Ranch around Laramie. Before they bought the ranch it was called Bull Mountain Ranch and laid right around the border of Colorado. I was staying in a cabin around the main ranch and I had an elk license. It also was deer season. So I shot an elk and dressed him out. I had to pack the elk only about 1 ½ miles. I had a whole bunch of beaver and coyotes I caught. I decided to go home. When I was driving out and opened the last gate there stood a four point (western count) buck. I knocked him down and went home with both my deer and elk. When I returned I caught a bunch of beaver, some coyotes, mink and muskrats and cats. I did pretty good there and stayed until the snow was too deep to navigate in the high winds. I pulled all the traps he could find and Dwight Mayland found the rest in the spring and gave them back to me. That was a good year especially when the prices were pretty good back then.

The Elk Fought Back

Jake knocked a great big six point elk (western count) down. He was kind of floundering around and Korell walked up to him to cut his jugular vein (to quicken his death) and he didn't want to mount him. He put a foot on the brow point on the ground and the elk came up with his head. He was so strong. He threw Jake ten or fifteen feet over his back. Korell landed way out in the sagebrush. Jake was sure glad that one of the horns hadn't gone in him. If he had had enough power he would have pushed it right through Jake. He could have killed Jake.

Game Warden

At dawn Jake was about three miles out of camp with a couple of hunters named John and Bones. They stumbled onto a herd of elk with two bulls in it. And the hunters each knocked a bull down. They asked Jake to get the pack horses while they dressed their elk out and hang them into a tree. Then we can all go to Jackson to celebrate. Jake returned with the pack horses and they packed their elk in. In Wyoming you have to leave either the horns or the bag on them to prove what sex the elk was. We got back to camp and hung up the elk. Those guys went into their tent and the game warden, Smith (not his real name), came riding in. He was kind of a fire and brimstone kind of guy. Smith always wanted to put a feather in his cap and Jake didn't like him because he was a mean little bastard. He asked why the bull elk don't have any sex on them. And Jake retorted, "How did you know they were bulls then?" Smith started blustering and saying that he always goes by the book. Jake replied that the peter hair and the smell was still there. And the horns are hanging there with them.

"If that isn't enough...." The game warden wouldn't let Jake finish the sentence and just kept saying that he went by the book. He asked who the guide was. Jake admitted that he was. The game warden wanted to see Jake's license and stuck it in his pocket. Jake told him that he hadn't dressed out the elk that the hunters had. And Jake offered to go get the hunters in the tent. But the game warden wouldn't let him go—told him to stay where he was. So he went over by the tent and asked to guys to come out because he had some questions for them. When the hunters came out he asked 'who dressed the elk.' And the hunters told the truth, 'We did.' Smith inquired where was the guide? He went after the pack horses, they assured him. Smith said that he was going to write the hunters a citation because you didn't leave any evidence of sex on the carcass. You will have to come in the morning to court in Jackson.

Jake spoke up and said he hadn't done anything wrong, 'give me back my license.' The game warden wasn't gonna, he just kept walking. Jake jumped in between him and his pickup and took off his jacket and just stood there and said, 'By God, I want my license back. You're not going to get back into the pickup until I get my license back.

The game warden growled, 'are you threatening me?' Korell replied that it wasn't a threat, it was just a promise. So Smith reached into his pocket and gave it back real reluctantly.

So the next day we went downtown and he listened to the warden's side and then Jake asked the judge if he could tell his side. The judge said, "That's what you are here for." Judge was a neat ol' guy, and Jake felt that the judge liked him. So Jake told him the whole story, 'These guys didn't realize that they were dressing the elk with out sex on them. But you could damn sure tell, there was enough of those long peter hairs and they stunk to high heaven – you could tell they were bulls.

The judge wrote a citation $40 for no sex. The game warden bellowed, "that's a $500 fine." The judge quietly replied, "Let me be the judge of that." Smith slunk out of there but Jake would sure have liked to hit him. The hunters showed that ticket all over Jackson. They couldn't stop laughing over getting a ticket for no sex.

Later on in the year Jerry and Schamber went hunting for themselves. Jake had just gotten his elk and packed it out. Jerry and Schamber both got their elk. Jerry was leading the horses out and he had put the elk on the horses. Schamber had to walk out, too, because Jerry had to put one of the elk on his horse.

Smith came by and asked whose elk is that? And Jerry replied that one was his and the other was his uncle's. Smith wanted to know where he was. Jerry informed him that he was suppose to take the elk back to camp and unload them and go back for him. The game warden ordered Jerry to wait right there until his uncle got there. Jerry explained that he couldn't walk very good and he was an old man. He stumbled a lot. I should go get him. Smith just insisted that Jerry wait right there and wouldn't relent. Finally, Schamber came in just a dragging. He was all played out. It's funny that he didn't have a heart attack. Jake felt he should have turned in that SOB for doing that. We would have even given him an extra horse to go with us to prove that everything was legal and right. He just wanted to be mean. He wouldn't listen. None of the guides trusted him. He is still up at Jackson and nobody likes him. Once while Jerry was guiding the game warden came across them and found out that the hunter hadn't signed his hunting license and that cost Jerry his guiding license for the rest of the season.

Out All Night

Jake was trailing a herd of elk in the snow and hadn't realized how late it had gotten. He had trailed them a long way—at least 15 miles from camp. He finally shot and dressed out the elk. Jake was about half way back to camp and it was pitch dark. He found where a hollow tree had fallen over and there was kinda of a nice cubby to crawl into. He dragged some firewood over and built a fire. Jake slept there until it started getting daylight. When he

got to camp Korell noticed that they were saddling up to look for him. Jake told them not to worry about him, that he was a survivor.

Target Shooting

Ray Randall and Jake were elk hunting. There were also some of Jake's neighbors from Pavillion and their relatives from back east in camp there. They were shooting at a quart tomato can target. They had it up there about 150 yards. They bet us $5.00 each. Raymond shot first and he drilled it right in the middle. Jake used the same gun as it was sighted in for 200 yards. Jake held down a little and hit it just about in the same hole. The other guys put their guns away – they never shot against Jake and Ray and gave each of them $5.00.

Overshoe Problem

Harold Brasie and Jake were going out to pack in elk. Korell was riding a bronc that hadn't been rode too much. He was leading a horse that was always pulling back. Jake had a dally on. They were just across the creek where it went straight up. The pack horse jerked back and pulled Jake's horse over. They were going straight up and it didn't take much to jerk him over. He slid back into the creek. Jake came off the horse. He wore a pair of overshoes. Generally he rides with cowboy boots but this day he had on work shoes and a heavy pair of overshoes. When he was upside down under that horse his foot was caught in the stirrup. The horse started splashing around and got up. He dragged Korell a ways. Jake finally kept pushing with his other foot and the overshoe came off. Boy, it was a good thing he was in the creek with steep banks and couldn't get out otherwise the horse would have dragged Jake to death. The horse finally found a lower place and he crawled out. Harold grabbed the reins. Jake tried to dry his clothes as much as he could. They went on and packed the elk out. That was a close one.

Elk Race

Jake was riding on a fast horse from the other side of Togwotee Pass going north over a great big meadow. The horse had run quite a few races. And to the left of the trail there was a high cliff with a long ridge that lasted about half a mile.

At the end of the ridge it curved back over to the trail. The only way that an animal could get down off the cliff was to hit that trail. So Jake saw an elk half way to the end and he raced over there. Jake got off and was kneeling and sure enough when the elk came around the bend; the cliff had guided him back down to the trail. When he started crossing the trail Jake knocked him down. That's the way he got his elk there. It was really quite exciting to race an elk. But Jake had won quite a lot of money racing his mare and knew that she could run.

Can Those Guys Hit Anything?

Jake was guiding for two guys from Alabama. Jake showed them a hella of nice bunch of elk as well as quite a few mule deer. They never hit nothing. They went home without any meat. The next year they came back and wanted Jake to guide them. But Jake balked. He didn't want them since they couldn't hit nothin'. Beck, the boss, came back and told Jake that the Alabamans said they would pay Jake a really good bonus. So Jake finally gave in.

Boy did Jake get a surprise! They left camp in the dark – just getting daylight. When they were only about 1 ½ miles from camp there was a big open meadow with a ridge and they could see the silhouette of a big bull elk walking that ridge. Jake was tying up his horse while one of the guys dropped his reins and shot. Jake thought he had missed again. But he was wrong. Jake walked over and found that he had killed a nice five point bull. Soon as the horns showed up in the skyline he pulled the trigger and he got him.

Jake dressed him out and rode back to camp. Clarence Beck asked why Jake was back in camp so soon. Jake told him that one of the guys had gotten an elk in the first meadow. Clarence and the lucky hunter packed the elk back to camp while Jake and the other hunter went on hunting.

They rode about 3 -4 miles and heard an elk bugling on a high peak. It was really steep there. They rode about another quarter mile and then tied their horses and walked. The elk was still bugling. Back and forth some others would answer. Jake walked up and parted some branches while the other guy had walked around the end. Just as Jake saw the elk the Alabaman shot. Down he went a nice six point bull. Jake couldn't believe it. Last year they couldn't hit anything. Now every time they shot something went down.

The next morning Jake packed that elk in. They had a ten day hunt and they had quite a few days left so Jake took them deer hunting. Same thing with the mule deer. The deer were a quarter mile away and they each knocked a deer down. Jake couldn't believe that they had changed that much.

So Jake asked why they couldn't hit beans last year. This year you never missed a shot.

They said that all summer long we had some of the guys working

for us roll truck tires down with cardboard signs. We would shoot with those bouncing tires rolling down the hill. In the fall when we got to drill the tires in the middle that's when we quit shooting and came hunting.

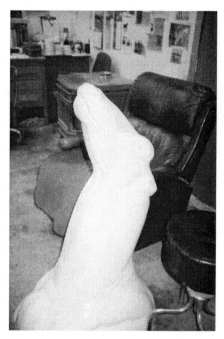

Fiber-glass form with all the muscles to mount an elk head.

Jake thought it sure made good shooters out of those guys. He was glad he took them then.

Swimming in the Ice

One evening in the '60's they were drinking in Beck's camp. There was ice on the edge of the creek. They were filling their jugs out of the creek and taking them into their tents for drinking water. Jake said that was just about cool enough to swim in. One guide, and Jake's son, Jerry, bet Jake that he wouldn't swim in there. Jake told them to lay their five bucks on that stump there. Jake undressed and broke the ice. They said he had to swim out to the log and back. And he did. He then went into the sleeping tent and wiped off and it really felt good to get warm clothes on. So they lost their $5. They kept drinking beer. There were a couple of Native American guys half Jake's age and they out weighed him. They wanted to arm wrestle and Jake put them both down. Then the whiskey started talking and Jake threw Jerry and Wayne and pinned them. Jake was getting a little tired by then and a little drunk. Jake said he could take both the guys down at the same time. Boy that was a big mistake. One of them grabbed Jake by the legs, another by the arms, and they popped Korell up and down on the ground. He was so sore and stiff the next day he could hardly get up.

Chapter Seven – Other Critters

The campfire snapped and crackled. Embers like golden feathers are carried gently away by the air currents or when pockets of sap explode the embers are forcefully shot upwards.

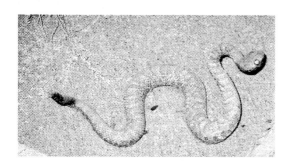

Bailing Rattlesnakes

When Jake was twelve he would ride along the dry land side of the canal with his friends. There was always a lot of snakes up there. They would curl up in the shade and we would start peppering them with our sling shots. They would have a pocket full of small rocks about the size of marbles. They'd pepper the snakes until they were dead.

A trapper's life changes dramatically in the summer months when fur is not prime. In Jake's case, farming becomes the number one priority. One summer afternoon he was baling hay. Due to a windstorm the previous evening, the hay was not being picked up by the baler properly. Jake got down off his tractor to kick some windrows into alignment. Jake left the baler running. The tractor was in neutral. Pretty soon Jake felt something on his pant leg. Looking down, he saw a big old rattler dangling from his Levi's leg. The snake's fangs had sunk into Jake's leg and then hung up in his pant leg. The snake had bitten Jake in the bone of his front leg. The fangs couldn't go in, but Jake still got some poison.

Kicking frantically and hopping about forced the snake to finally come loose. As a child he remembered seeing the family dog laying in blue mud after being bitten by a rattler. Jake decided to do the same. He sat down in the shade by the ditch bank, squeezed the poison out, and packed the wound with mud. After resting for awhile, he finished baling the rest of his hay before going home.

He told his wife what had happened. Frantic, Martha pleaded with him to see a doctor.

He said, "It's okay, the snake died." However, Jake was pretty sick for three or four days. Jake never went to the doctor or anything. The only shot he received was a shot of

Johnny Red Walker Scotch Whiskey.

Sure enough, Jake had killed not only the snake that bit him but one of his buddies as well.

Deer Hunters

Jerry Spence, the lawyer, had a ranch up by Dubois back in the '60's. There is a bunch of timber and a bunch of mule deer in there. I had two hunters' deer hunting in an old Jeep. They walked to the edge, knelt down and started shooting. Nothing happened. And I thought, damn! There were a four bucks standing up there and they were just milling around. They just kept banging away. I shot two of them and put my gun away and the hunters thought they had killed them and I never told them any different. They claimed them.

Trapping and Hunting Bear

While trapping black bears is currently illegal in Wyoming, in the days when it used to be lawful, Walt Disney bought a piece of ground up above Dubois, Wyoming. The guy by the name of Miller married Walt Disney's daughter took care of the place and hired Jake to take care of the black bears that were killing Walt

Disney's angus cattle. Joe York, who worked there, and Korell teamed together.

We took a chain saw and some rotten elk meat from a freezer that quit and put it in a pannier. We took a number five black bear trap and we rode up into the Dunoir valley where the bear was killing cattle on the summer range and made a cubby about five feet long, three feet wide and three feet high with logs and bumped it up against a great big tree. Threw some of the rotten meat back into the end and set the trap back in the cubby where elk, cattle and people couldn't step in that trap. We had it bolted to about a nine foot log.

The law was when setting a bear trap with clamps you had to have that clamp release wired in the tree within reach so that if a man did step in it he could let himself out. Within five days we had that bear and that stopped the killing and we made a rug out of him that is up in Hollywood.

Another time Jake and Martha were riding up by Beauty Park with two friends. They glassed a black bear eating on a dead cow. Jake doesn't think the bear killed the cow, but that she had died from eating that poisoning larkspur because she was all bloated. At a certain stage the purple larkspur is poisonous. It will kill a cow if she eats enough of it. Jake snuck up to 100 yards of the bear. He took off when Jake hit him. Jake felt he had hit him pretty good. But he got into a washout and Jake walked along the bank up above. Korell could hear him breathing. Pretty soon he couldn't hear him breathing. So Jake walked down a ways and walked into that gully. The bear charged to within five feet of Jake. Jake shot his 06 and finished him off.

Blood Shirt

Jake had a moose hunter and the two of them had hunted pretty hard. Korell wondered out loud if the guy was looking for a trophy or just something to eat. The hunter replied that this was his first moose and that he would rather have a two year old rather than a big tough one. They call a two year old a mature moose. So he killed this nice two year old and he didn't want him mounted.

So Jake dressed him out. He cut his jugular vein and when the blood hit the white snow it looked really pretty. Jake said it looked good enough to eat.

The hunter said he'd bet Jake a new shirt that you won't drink any of that blood.

So Jake took his hands and caught two handfuls and he drank the blood. And he was all bloody in the front.

The hunter shook his head. "You scavenger son of gun. I didn't think you would do that. I have a shirt that is still in the wrapper and you are the same size that I am going to have to give you that good wool shirt now."

So when we got back to camp Ruth Beck was cooking and she was worried when she asked what happened.

The hunter replied that Jake was a scavenger and drank some moose

blood and now he owed him a new shirt. And the hunter went into his tent and got a new shirt still wrapped and he tossed it to him.

Boy, that was a good shirt from a Woolen Mills (could be Pendleton). Jake wore that shirt for years. Never could wear it out. One day Martha washed it in warm water and it shrunk and Jake couldn't wear it again. We had this little bitty guy that was working for us and Jake gave the shirt to him. He finally wore it out.

Moose in Wind River Heritage Center

Moose Attacked Horse

There was this big moose that had a real big set of antlers on him. It was during the rutting season.

Jake was bringing a pack string out and had moose horns tied on this black horse. That moose came running over and attacked that black horse with those antlers. He ran a horn into the horses shoulder pretty deep.

So Jake jumped off and shot that moose in the horns. It was a 60" spread through the horns. The shot knocked him down, but Jake didn't want to kill him because he didn't have a moose license.

58

Jake rode off and when he looked back the moose was staggering and running back into the timber.

But Jake couldn't use that horse for about a week and only after Korell had doctored him with some horse medicine.

Markets direct trappers to different species, and Jake spent a number of years trapping the high mountains on snowshoes for marten. Some of his trapline cabins were simple, and he spent many evenings cut off from the world in dugout cabins. His wife was very understanding about him being gone on his trapline for a month or more at a time, "At first I was worrying, and after a while I didn't worry anymore because I know Jake's a survivor," Martha remarked.

Family Fishing

Jake's son, Lee was a paraplegic because of polio. When he was a teenager the whole family went on a fishing/camping trip at Jake's hunting camp. Lee stayed in camp while the others walked along a stream to fish. Lee heard some noise and looked up to see a black bear. The bear snooped around in every tent. Lee kept shooting in the air. Lee

got the bear to leave but then he would come right back again. Finally when the family returned to camp the bear was around the horses. The horses all tore loose. Jake had to go run down the horses, but it wasn't too hard because some of them were hobbled. The ones that weren't hobbled were dragging ropes. Jake caught up with them about three miles from camp. About the time Jake brought them back he heard two shots and J. Bob White, one of the guides that was helping to take care of these other fishermen had shot the bear. The fisherman hadn't returned to camp and so Jake dragged the bear into their sleeping tent and laid him in the doorway. Jake propped his mouth wide open. When one of the fishermen threw back the tent flaps he jumped back. But he didn't say anything so they pulled the same joke on three or four other ones. They all got that big surprise. White mounted that bear life size later on. It wasn't too bad a fur.

Martha and Jake fishing in Mexico

Ling Fishing

In the late '40's and early '50's Jake was fishing on Ocean Lake. At that time Ocean Lake was full of Ling.

They were so thick that there was no limit on them. You could run as many as twenty lines at one time and it was nothing to get 18 ling on 20 lines. Jake used chalk line with a big hook and minnow. In the winter Jake would stack them on the ice like cordwood and then go around and give them to the neighbors. Jake kept his neighbors in fish. That Ocean Lake has come and gone, there aren't too many ling out there any more. The lake got full of carp and they ate the ling and their eggs. (The Wyoming record ling fish weighed 19 lbs. 4 oz.) Jake caught his largest fish in Montana – an 85 pound paddle fish.

Jake makes these drums for the Native Americans in the area. He hollows out a cottonwood tree.

Jake mounted the buffalo (above) and made the bull boat (left) from another buffalo hide pictured above. Mountain men would string several of these waterproof bull boats together to make a parade going down a river carrying the trapper, and his beaver hides.

60

Chapter Eight – Bobcats, Lynx and Mountain Lions

The campfire's light has faded but still radiates warmth. Long, thin tendrils of fire flow with the wind and then disappear.

Good Shooting

One time George Hinkle and George Haines went on a bobcat hunt with my hounds, Jake recalls. These guys lived out west of Riverton, Wyoming, near where I lived and I used to hunt quite a little and fished out of a boat with them on Dinwoody Lake. They were really good on target practice. Boy, nobody could beat them. They hit every target and could drive nails with their guns.

They could outshoot me on a target but when we went hunting and were running game, I could outshoot them. I pretty much hit everything I shot at. When they got back to the pickup after running the hounds they were shooting at tin cans and were waiting for me. I told them that aint shooting. I lined up some 22 shells on a stick. I was popping those shells off at 30 yards with my 22 rifle. Then I bent over and shot upside down. After that

they didn't shoot with me any more that day. Those guys told this story a lot times and the story was all around town.

Trapping Cats

Generally in the same area as bobcats there will be mountain lions. But they will be in the rock ridges. Female bobcats with kittens generally stay in the ledges and trees where they can get away from the coyotes because coyotes will kill the kittens. And the male can go anyplace because even two coyotes couldn't kill an old tom. Coyotes will leave the toms alone and kill the kittens. You trap a bobcat a little differently than you do coyotes and foxes. You can make a cubby of rocks to guide him in and put your scent way back and put the trap at the mouth of the cubby. Or you can use a walk thru set between two boulders with a path through them.

At the time the book is being published Jake is selling the stretchers he makes (pictured left) for $10 plus shipping.

Put a little scent on both sides of the boulders and set that trap in between the two boulders.

Besides buying and preparing furs, Korell sells some trapping supplies. "We don't have everything,

but we have enough for what people want and ask for," he claims. Like a lot of professional trappers, Jake makes his own lures. During the early '30's he was given the formula by Roy Hyer, a ranch hand trapper who worked the off season on his father's ranch. It was a good recipe, and Jake still makes this lure, along with some others that he has created through the years.

Jake with his dogs and 50 pound bobcat–the biggest one he ever caught.

If he likes you he make give or sell you some, but if he doesn't than you won't get any. Jake uses a little cat urine, catnip and sweet ainse with his scent lure made with the rotten afterbirth and fish or skunk smell. You will get him every time with that kind of a setup.

Cats have really good eyes that he can see in either night or daytime. So a cat hunts everything by sight. He doesn't have a good nose and you can't pull him from very far. So about two feet off the ground Jake puts up a flag attractor; of a piece of jackrabbit fur or a piece of hide off a sheep with a piece of bail wire and just a little light breeze will wave that back and forth. And the cat will go over and investigate and work the scent and you can catch him every time.

Raw Shooting

In the '60's, Jake and Jerry, his son were following two 'coon hounds chasing a bobcat track. They had almost got across the river when Jake stepped on a thin spot in the ice and broke through. Jake was hanging onto his shotgun and hollered at Jerry and he turned around and came running. Jerry shoved a long pole that the water had knocked down and he pulled his father out. Jake was soaked through. It was about ten or fifteen below that day. Jerry built a fire and Jake put some bark and leaves down and brushed the snow away to stand on. Korell wringed out his clothes and then put them by the fire to dry. Pretty soon the dogs started barking a little ways away. The wind had come up and they lost the bobcat track. But the dogs all had been sniffing around and they now all opened up and treed. So Jake slipped into his slushy over shoes and stark naked walked around the corner to watch the dogs barking under the tree. Pretty soon

one of them came backing out of there with a big 'coon in his mouth. It was the first 'coon Jake saw in Fremont County. He didn't even know there was 'coon down there. Dogs killed the 'coon and Jerry started yelling at his father to get back to the fire. By that time his clothes were dry enough to put on and so they went on hunting.

Jake uses a plastic garbage bag for a disposable apron when fleshing out a hide.

You can't trap mountain lions but you can run them with dogs during the season with a permit. Or if you see one in the open, which isn't very often, you can shoot them.

In 2003 the bobcat prices came back good. The rest of the fur prices never came back that much. They are about $300-$400 again. Right today the cat prices are holding up real good. But will there be any trappers out there with $3.00 gas prices – they can't even afford to trap any more unless you get a little extra for doing predator work.

Jake says that will make it through the difficulties of the fur business. The two also make leather coats from their tanned hides. "We've had a few bad years, but we've managed to hang in there when other outfits haven't," he says. "We've been able to average the good years with the bad ones and come out just fine."

In the '70's Jake had some coon hounds that would run bobcats. It was nothing to catch between 2 – 5 cats a day between the dogs and traps. It was really good between the 1978 to 1988 in the crash. (The energy fields in Wyoming went bust.) The stocks and bonds and fur prices all went down almost to nothing.

Guiding Business

How did you ever start this guiding business?" the weathered man asked Jake as he threw another log on the fire.

Jake was guiding for some outfitters. He was a good guide, got everyone their meat. Jake figured if he was going to have a little spare time that he might as well get into some thing that would raise more money to help his family. So he went to the game and fish and the forest service. Between the two they will give you a designated area. That's the way that Jake got a camp. Jake's first camp was in the Dunoir Valley. He was in there for a long time. Percy Yarborough kinda wanted Jake out of there because it fit in with the Diamond G. So they moved Jake over to Togwotee Pass around Two Ocean Mountain. Later on he moved over to Brooks Lake. Jake always ran a good clean camp. Most of the hunters got their elk. Most of the time Jake had four hunters in camp at a time; mostly non residents – but sometimes one or two residents. Jake never had over six hunters at his camp at one time. Korell was making money and it helped buy their farm. Martha and Jerry helped. Two other guys worked as wranglers. The hunting season in Wyoming goes from about the middle of September to the middle of November. Then Jake would come home and start trapping. The fur was good and prime by then. It all helped. The hunters paid Jake really good and fur prices were up. Gas was cheap enough that you could make money. Jake was an outfitter for 27 years.

It got so that hunters had to draw for an area. Some of Jake's hunters came year after year for fifteen to twenty years. The same guys over and over again. Then they had to draw and Jake couldn't keep his camp full. Some years he would get more than he wanted and some years he would hardly get any. Then Jake got tired of baby sitting for the town guys. You have to have a lot of patience and Jake felt he never had enough of that. He'd bite his tongue a lot of times.

The guys that bought Brooks Lake Lodge bought his outfit, horses, tents, sleeping bags and everything. They gave him a good price, too. They also paid him a little for his campsite, too.

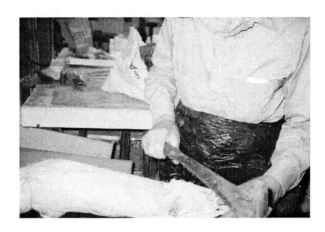

Buying and Selling Furs

Jake had been buying furs since 1970. In 1981-82 season Korell bought over $500,000 worth of furs from local trappers. When the bottom went out of the market he lost $30,000. But he made up the loss in the next two years and then got out of the business. He says you have to average the years; one bad year in fifteen is not all that bad. Hides are priced according to size, color and quality. Purchases vary from under $10 for muskrat pelts to over $200 for bobcat furs. If the whole carcass is brought Jake deducts $15 for skinning. He annually presents a workshop to teach beginning trappers how to set a trap as well as the ethics of trapping, skinning and proper fur care.

One time he knew that some Arapahos were bring some pelts for him to buy. He knew that they would have trouble cashing a check so he went into town to get $30,000 in cash. He noticed that someone followed him out of the bank and that a car pursued him all the way to his ranch. He raced into the shed where he did his taxidermy and got his 45 pistol. When the guy opened the door Jake level the gun at him and asked if he could help him. The guy just shook his head and mumbled and left. Jake called the cops and they picked him and found out he was wanted for bank robbery in another state.

Stealing, he states is a major problem. Also, trappers need to know when to pull out of an area. "Trapping plays a big part in animal control. If done properly, it protects animal populations. I don't believe in extinction. When I am trapping in an area where the animals are showing signs of losing too many numbers, then I pull up and move on. I have trapped some of the same areas for 35 years and there have been no problems. Animals just have to be harvested with sense," Jake advises. He stress that proper handling of the furs, with as few cuts as possible makes it a good fur, and more valuable. He instructs them that they are trying hard not to buy any bobcat furs since the animals are becoming increasingly rare. Jake is not for pushing the cats even though the prices of each fur may go up the number of cats may go down and he wants an ongoing profit besides being able to see them around. Fox and coyotes are the most popular furs and Jake

with his son Jerry buy more of them than any other animal. He used to get as many foxes as coyotes, but now their numbers are dwindling and they get about half as many. He states that this information has increased the quality of the furs available. "The trapping life has been a good one," Korell asserts, "and the fur business is a good one—half my living, and I like it or I wouldn't be doing it. My heart is in it."

Talk to anyone who knows Jake well, from game wardens to fellow trappers, and they will tell you what a fine conservationist he is. When a particular species is being over-hunted or over-trapped in an area, he informs the Wyoming Game and

Jake teaches trappers how to best prepare the hides for sale. If furs aren't properly handled, they can be worthless.

66

Fish as well as trappers. Due to his reputation as a knowledgeable wildlife expert, his advice is taken seriously. He understands the Wyoming ecosystem and takes the time to educate others through his many educational workshops and demonstrations. People often comment that "Jake is part animal himself".

How to Prepare the Skins for the Most Money

If the animal has fleas Jake sprays them with flea spray and ten minutes later every flea that's on them is dead.

When Jake skins an animal he hangs it by one leg to get the part between the legs. He also likes to start to get the belly part before hanging by two legs. On the back legs cut an incision from the rectum to the paw. Make an incision on each foreleg from the paw to the elbow – it helps when you are pulling the hide off right on off until it tears at the paw or you cut it at any length you need.

Mostly work the hide loose with your fingers to prevent cuts; Jake only uses his knife around the ears and eyes.

When you prepare the animal; take the glands on either side of the rectum. Then a white pea that's also there. Then there is a button in the throat (one on each side) and also the butt of the ear is also a good gland to put in your lure. Jake also takes the bladder and part of the gut that has skat in it to use as lures.

First thing Jake does after he gets him skinned is to wash the fur with a little bit of detergent and rinse with cold water. This gets all the blood and dirt out of the hide. Before he is plumb dry Jake uses sinew to sew up the holes with a baseball stitch. You start at one end and when you turn it over you can't even tell its there. After Korell sews them up you can't hardly tell where there was any holes. Then it will go in with the #1 coyotes. Foxes and bobcats have fine fur and washing them doesn't work. The fur isn't right afterwards. You need to just brush them with a wire brush after they are cured and the blood and dirt comes right out.

When you first put a coyote on a stretcher, place the skin side out and leave it that way overnight until it glazes over. That way they won't stick to the wooden stretcher.

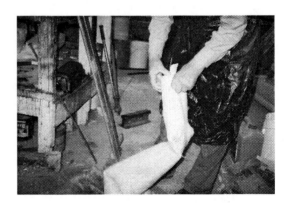

The next day the hide is generally soft enough to turn but to keep from tearing you start on the nose end. If you start to turn it from the tail end you will tear the hide. If you start at the face and turn it backwards they never tear. Keep turning this way until it is completely turned, do not reach up inside from the bottom as this causes tears in the hide. That's a secret that Jake found out for himself. It really works. This is one of his shortcuts that other trappers don't know. See how easy it is to turn a glazed hide. Start on the small end and the large end is really loose. (Coyote and bobcat are prepared the same way.)

After the hide is tacked down you can spread the stretcher to the width you need. If you stretch the hide too big it will look thin and of poor quality. Get the tightness by the size of the stretcher you have. Leave a little slack for the dryness. It should be just barely taut. You can feel when you get it to the size. Stretchers have to be the right size for the animal. After putting the hide on the stretcher you need to fluff it up and comb it all out and be ready for sale.

Jake puts a little of the Show Sheen for horses on the dried fur and tumbles them in a commercial clothes dryer with some ground corn cob meal. (Jerry has welded a heavy tin frame around it so the ground

corn cob meal won't fall out.) They come out beautiful, fluffy and shiny. They bring more money. The fur buyers go by what they see and that's how they pay.

Martha and Jake won 1st place in the parade float pictured above. Martha stood steadfast behind Jake and enjoyed attending mountain man festivities with her husband and trading fur. She is well known for her mild manner and wonderful sense of humor, which is necessary being married to a man like Jake for almost 70 years.

Jake's trapping line cabin

Legacy

If Jake had his whole life to live over again the only thing that he would like to change is that his wife, Martha wouldn't have to work so hard in the beet fields when they were first married. She was really a hard worker and he didn't force her to do it. But he wishes he could have provided a little bit better. They tended 22 acres for the Haun's which is quite a little bit for just a couple to do.

Recently, Korell's stock broker told him that he had enough money to live the way he wanted to for fifteen years. Jake wonders what he would do then. Currently he wants to get the Wind River Heritage Center moved over to the site on Federal Avenue and have the trappers and homesteader's cabins moved there and fixed up the way they would have been in their heyday. And also move in horse drawn farming and mining equipment. Please contact the Wind River Heritage Center if you would like to help with this project.

Jake continues to trap in 2005 as this is being written. Currently he has 100 traps in his trapline. He has been referred to as the "rancher's best friend". He has been called upon many times through the years to trap coyotes and foxes that were killing calves and lambs. He has even bagged mountain lions that were stalking mare and foals.

The coals of the fire are glowing dim. The wind has died and the thermometer is dropping. Time to snuggle into your sleeping bag to dream of your next hunting or trapping adventure.

Attachments

Photo taken by Bob Peck, courtesy Riverton Ranger

TRAPPER JAKE'S AWARDS AND ACHIEVEMENTS

Jake has successfully trapped all species of furbearers and predators in Wyoming during his career. He started running his trap line on foot at the age of seven. As his trap line grew, he graduated to running his trap line on horseback. During the 1970's, he started using a snowmobile; and now, at the age of 91, he uses a four-wheel drive pickup with plenty of walking as any successful trapper knows. He still does. Since he began trapping at the age of seven. Jake Korell has trapped most of Wyoming, into Colorado on the south side, into Idaho on the west side, and into Montana on the north side. A breakdown of the areas worked follows:

- Park County near Powell, Wyoming Muskrats and Skunks

- Rawhide Creek near Lingle, Wyoming Muskrats, Skunks, Ermine, Badgers, and Mink

- North Platte River between Lingle and Fort Laramie, Wyoming Muskrats, Skunks, Ermine, Badgers, Mink, Beaver, Bobcats, Raccoon, and Coyotes

- All of Fremont County, Wyoming

- All of Sweetwater County, Wyoming Muskrats, Mink, Skunks, Civet Cats, Beaver, Badgers, Bobcats, Coyotes, Fox, Raccoon, Bear, and Mountain Lions

- Albany County near Laramie, Wyoming Coyotes, Bobcats, Badgers, Raccoon, Mink and Muskrat

- Teton County near Jackson Hole, Wyoming Pine Marten and Coyote

- Crook County near Sundance, Wyoming Beaver and Coyotes

CONTRIBUTIONS TO LOCAL, DISTRICT STATE & NATIONAL ORGANIZATIONS

- LIFETIME MEMBER OF NATIONAL TRAPPERS ASSOCIATION -- member Trappers Hall of Fame

- MEMBER OF WYOMING TRAPPERS ASSOCIATION. Helped organize and start the Wyoming association. Hosted the 1990 state convention in Riverton, Wyoming.

- MEMBER OF 1838 RENDEZVOUS ASSOCIATION Conducts trapping and fur handling workshops each summer at the rendezvous Plays the part of Jim Bridger in skits performed by the association.

- Plays mountain man music on his mouth harp, participates in black powder shooting events, tomahawk throwing contests, etc. Sets up display booth of his tanned fur and trapping paraphernalia.

- MEMBER OF NATIONAL RIFLE ASSOCIATION

- MEMBER OF WYOMING OUTFITTERS ASSOCIATION ~ Licensed guide and outfitter for 26 years in the Wind River Mountains of Wyoming.

- MEMBER OF AMERICAN QUARTER HORSE ASSOCIATION

- HORSE RACING STEWARD AT MEADOWLARK DOWNS FOR 3 YEARS

- FREMONT COUNTY FAIR HORSE SUPERINTENDENT FOR 14 YEARS ~ Helped many 4-H and FFA youth with their horse projects.

- PAST PRESIDENT OF THE RIVERTON RIDING CLUB

- HONORARY MEMBER OF RIVERTON FFA CHAPTER ~

Sponsored and chaperoned many FFA events and trips.

- LICENSED WYOMING TAXIDERMIST FOR 25 YEARS – and still does his own

- LIFELONG MEMBER OF TRINITY LUTHERAN CHURCH ~ Served on Children's Christmas Committee for 4 years.

- DONOR TO THE RIVERTON MUSEUM

- BOARD MEMBER WIND RIVER HERITAGE CENTER

- MAJOR DONOR WIND RIVER HERITAGE CENTER

CONTRIBUTIONS TO TRAPPER EDUCATION

<u>RAW FUR WORKSHOPS SINCE</u> 1980, Jake and his son, Jerry, have been conducting free workshops on trapping and proper fur handling. Jake has taught many students, including members of the Arapahoe and Shoshone Indian tribes, how to use scent and lures, make sets, and care for fur. For the past three years, he has been presenting his workshop at the 1838 Rendezvous held in Riverton, Wyoming, each summer.

<u>FEDERAL WILDLIFE CONVENTION</u> Jake was invited to speak at the Federal Wildlife meeting held in Thermopolis, Wyoming. He shared his lifetime trapping experiences and outstanding knowledge of Wyoming wildlife and gave demonstrations on trapping, skinning, and tanning fur.

<u>ELEMENTARY SCHOOL EDUCATION</u> "Trapper Jake" has made countless appearances at elementary schools throughout Fremont County, Wyoming. Dressed in buckskins, he has charmed youngster with tales of his trapping experiences. His educational speeches explain that "trapping should be done right or not at all". He gives demonstrations on how to set traps and handle fur and explains that fur is "a renewable resource". His most recent appearances have been enjoyed by students at Wind River Elementary School at Pavillion, Wyoming; Jackson Elementary School in Riverton, Wyoming; Shoshoni Elementary School, Shoshoni, Wyoming; Saint Stephen's Indian Mission School at St. Stephens, Wyoming; Ashgrove Elementary School at Riverton, Wyoming; and Arapahoe School at Arapahoe, Wyoming.

<u>ONE-ON-ONE TRAINING</u> Since 1960 Jake has taken two lucky youngsters between the ages of 10 and 14 as full-time students. Each year he chooses two new novices to run a trap line with him and learn how to make sets, skin fur and handle it properly. He also teaches them the fine art of making scents, which. He refers to as his "Avon Collection", to lure different species of furbearers.

Many of the professional trappers in Fremont County were once Jake's students.

TRAPPING VIDEOS Members of the 1838 Rendezvous Association have made educational videos of Jake trapping beaver, bobcats, fox, and coyotes. The beaver video features Jake's replica of an 1838 beaver press, which he built himself. The videos give step-by-step instruction on trapping, skinning, and handling of pelts.

CONTRIBUTIONS TO THE TRAPPING FIELD

RAW FUR BUYER Jake has been buying fur directly from trappers since 1970. He has a reputation of always being honest and fair.

ANTIQUE TRAP COLLECTOR SINCE the age of seven Jake has collected over 400 antique traps, representing 15 different companies dating back to the early 1800's. He has a complete Newhouse collection on display at his museum located on Fremont Street in Riverton, Wyoming. The rest of his collection is on display at the Riverton Museum and at his home.

1838 RENDEZVOUS ASSOCIATION Jake is a member of the 1838

Rendezvous Association. Jake (3rd from left) and friends at 1838 Rendezvous. Founded in 1989 for the express purpose of preserving a rare historical landmark, the 1838 Rendezvous Association continues working toward that goal. Mountain men left no physical trace of their lives upon the western landscape and this site is dedicated to the men, women and children who moved so lightly upon the world that only the land and the river remain as a witness to those shining times. In 1830 and 1838, this great "summer fair in the mountains" was held at the confluence of the Big and Little Wind Rivers, near present-day Riverton, Wyoming. This event is held over the 4th of July each year.

Jake plays the part of Jim Bridger in their skits.

ACHIEVEMENTS AND ACCOMPLISHMENTS MADE IN THE TRAPPING FIELD

SEARS AND ROEBUCK AWARD One of the first awards Jake ever received was in 1946 for being the best fur handler.

CITIZEN CRIME STOPPER AWARD When Jake was approached to buy some raw fur that he believed was stolen, he contacted the Fremont County Sheriff. Together, they set up a sting operation. As a result, Jake and his son, Lee, were awarded the Citizen Crime Stopper Award for successfully solving a crime and helping to apprehend the criminal. See attached copy of newspaper clipping.

BRONZE SCULPTURE In 1985, Artist Gary Shoop sculpted a bronze of Jake and named it "Jake/1985". It depicts Jake on snowshoes with traps in hand and carrying a rifle. The bronze is an exact likeness of Jake running his trap lines in his badger coat, leather leggings, and beaver cap. See attached copy of newspaper clipping.

MAGAZINE ARTICLE IN *"VOICE OF THE TRAPPER"* An article, "Lifer Jake Korell," appeared in the 1987 spring issue of *Voice of the Trapper*.

BOOK COVER Jake is featured with his horse packed with beaver pelts on the cover of the book, *Rendezvous on the Wind, Plenty of Trade, Whiskey and White Women* by Lavinia Dobler and Loren Jost.

MAPPING VIDEOS Jake has starred in videos which have been aired on television to promote the annual 1838 Rendezvous celebration in Riverton each summer. The videos feature Jake doing step-by-step instruction on trapping, skinning and processing beaver, bobcats, fox and coyotes.

MOUNTAIN MAN MUSIC AWARDS For two consecutive years, Jake has won awards at the 1838 Rendezvous for playing old-time music on his harmonica while dancing a jig.

WYOMING GOVERNOR'S AWARD At the Fort Bridger Rendezvous in 1991, Wyoming Governor Mike Sullivan presented Jake with a medal for trapping the most years of anyone in the state.

JAKE KORELL SHOOTING RANGE In 1992, Jake was honored by the 1838 Rendezvous Association when they named a shooting range for him at the original site of the 1838 rendezvous.

JAKE KORELL SHOOTING CONTEST In recognition of Jake's rugged lifestyle and prowess with a rifle, the 1838 Rendezvous Association named a shooting contest after him. The event is held each summer during the 1838 Rendezvous celebration.

78

THE WHITE HOUSE
WASHINGTON

Congratulations and best wishes for an enjoyable birthday celebration. May your day be filled with happy memories, bright hopes, and the love of family and friends.

Sincerely,

Jake's 90th birthday card from the President and Laura Bush

ELLIS ISLAND
1892–1992

TM © 1987 SLEIF, INC

The Statue of Liberty-Ellis Island Foundation, Inc.

proudly presents this

Official Certificate of Registration

in

THE AMERICAN IMMIGRANT WALL OF HONOR

to officially certify that

The Henry Korell Family

came to the United States of America from

Argentina

joining those courageous men and women who came to this country in search of personal
freedom, economic opportunity and a future of hope for their families.

*Interim stays were made in Russia and Argentina but language, cus-
toms and culture remained German.

Lee A. Iacocca
The Statue of Liberty-Ellis Island
Foundation, Inc.

LIBERTY
1886·1986

© © 1982 SLEIF, INC

(left) Jake with Lone Soldierwolf (Northern Arapaho)

Jake is well respected by both tribes of the Wind River Reservation. They say he is white on the outside and red on the inside—he sees both sides of the problem. Many of them bring their pelts for Jake to buy. One of the greatest tributes Jake has ever received was from a member of the Shoshone Indian tribe. Jake has managed to break through the barrier known as Indian humor. He is fondly known on the Wind River Indian Reservation as "Silly Jake" or "Crazy Jake". The respect Jake has gained from residents of the reservation was revealed when he was politely asked if an eagle feather could be placed in his coffin by tribal members when he dies. This honor is rarely, if ever, bestowed on white men. The significance of the feather placed in the coffin is to ensure that the recipient will "soar with the eagles".

Wind River Heritage Center

Jake's idea for a Mountain Man Fur Trade Exploring the West Museum began to take shape in about 1990 during meetings of the 1838 Mountain Man Association. Jake was one of the founders and a major donor for the Wind River Heritage Center. Known not only as a skilled trapper, Jake has gained fame as a big game hunter and taxidermist. His collection of all the furbearers and big game animals of Wyoming, mounted life-size, are on display at his free Center in Riverton, Wyoming. Jake and his son, Jerry, harvested all of the animals themselves and did all of the taxidermy work. Dedicated to preserving the natural and human history of the West the Center also has a collection of historic, traps dating from 1804, from the fur trade era. The Korell Collection specializes in Wyoming wildlife including big-game species, predators and fur bearers. Bison, bears and grey wolves are among the most popular exhibits. Colorful dioramas depicting the animals' natural habitat serve as backdrops for the mounts.

Wildlife plays an important role in the Wind River Valley. The area has always been a prized hunting ground. Historically, wild animals provided meat, fur, bones, hides, horns, and even teeth. Today, they continue to be valued both for their aesthetic appeal and for their meat and hides. The Center displays provide a dose-up look at these animals that have been so vital in the settling of the American West.

The Center also sponsors slide shows, lectures and Native American dancing demonstrations throughout the year. Wind River Heritage Center personnel presents on-site mountain man, trapper and/or furs, programs to groups including school class, Boy Scouts, Girl Scouts, and various community organizations. There were visitors from 44 states and 7 foreign countries at the museum during 2004.

In addition to its wildlife displays, the Center houses an extensive gift store specializing in Native American art and jewelry. Locally made beadwork and leather goods-trademarks of the Eastern Shoshone and Northern Arapaho tribes that inhabit the Wind River Indian Reservation-can be purchased a the store. Plans for the new building are being pursed with construction planned for late 2005 or early 2006 at the old Knight Theatre site on South Federal Boulevard, Riverton, Wyoming.

Fifty golden years

The Story of Jake and Martha Korell

BY JANE KORELL MALLER

On April 22nd, it seems,
In Nineteen Hundred and Fourteen,
Jacob Korell was born in Lincoln,
With a grin and eyes a-twinkling.

In the merry month of May,
On the 12th, the very day,
Martha Gradwohl made the scene
In Nineteen Hundred Seventeen.

Destined by God's will and grace,
They'd meet someday face to face.
Weekend nights were made for dancing.
Soon they met and were romancing.

Martha had a beauty rare,
A lovely smile and raven hair.
Jake was Mr. Right,
A handsome man, her shining knight.

All their brothers, and sisters too.
Watched and smiled as true love grew.
Even sexy Sloppy Socks
Couldn't beat Mart, the lady fox.

In '36 on March the 9th,
Jake took Martha for his wife.
They eloped and Gradwohl's sighed.
True love won! The knot was tied!

To Riverton they did go
In '37 to earn some dough.
They worked the Haun farm for a year,
Then bought a place out near Kinnear.

A place to finally call their own
On which some seed crops could be grown.
In '38 their dreams came true –
Acres of SAGEBRUSH for those two!

From dawn 'til dusk the two did toil
To break the sagebrush from the soil.
Many a seed these two did sow.
Alfalfa and grass soon did grow.

They built a house of straw and loam.
Adobe bricks made their first home.
Sheep and cattle and horses grazed,
And lambs and calves and foals were raised.

In September of '38,
The 21st the very date,
Came a bouncing baby boy
Whom proud parents named Lee Roy.

Four years later, time just flew –
September 4th of '42—
The stork brought little Gerald Gene.
No cuter babe was ever seen.

Six years later in '48,
The 3rd of May, the precise date,
Martha Jane became a daughter
To a loving mom and father.

These were tough times, hard and lean.
Dollars were few and far between.
They laughed and loved and shed some tears
And somehow made it through the years.

Their love together did not fade
For Martha out of Jacob made
A husband full of fun and cheer
Who fished and trapped and hunted deer.

Then in 1951,
Polio struck Lee, their son.
Doctors, nurses, woe and strife
Were his destiny in life.

Every autumn until '62,
The outfitting business they did do.
Clients got the best of care
While hunting elk and deer and bear.

They moved to Riverton again.
Fate had changed what might have been.
Taxidermy and guiding dudes,
All were done to provide food.

Martha cleaned for those in town.
She did her share without a frown.
They did their best to make ends meet,
And there was always enough to eat.

The horse trade was another way
To have some fun and earn some pay.
Always ready for a race,
They loved the thrill – win, show or place.

They have some memories quite sad:
The loss of parents and kin they had.
For brothers and sisters they still grieve.
'Twas sad to see their loved ones leave.

They raised their children up with morals
To worship God and not to quarrel.
They tried to teach them right from wrong,
And to be honest, tough and strong.

Through the years, the family grew.
Scott Maller said to Jane, "I do."
Jerry took Iva for his wife
To share the ups and downs of life.

Jake built Mart a brand new home,
Made with love from wood and stone.
They made a living off the land,
Then sold it for a price quite grand.

After forty-six years of marriage,
Came a grandchild's baby carriage.
Kathy Lee was found inside
To fill grandparents' hearts with pride.

In '84 when Jake fell ill,
Martha's eyes with tears did fill.
She thought her heart would surely break
To lose her spouse and best friend, Jake.

To God they turned in thoughtful prayer,
A gift He gave them, one quite rare.
Doctors with their special skills
Fixed Jake's heart and cured his ills.

Broken hearts can still be mended
If special care they're tended.
Blessed were they, with God's great care,
To have each other's lives to share.

Hard work, giggles, joy and tears,
All were shared throughout the years.
Their sense of humor and German pride
Made a success of things they tried.

To Jake and Martha, here's a toast:
For fifty years you've made the most
Of what life had for you in store.
Here's hoping you share fifty more.

Written with love and gratitude for Mom and Dad in
celebration of your Golden Wedding Anniversary.
From your daughter, Jane

A Resolution
Of the Members of the Senate of the
Fifty-sixth Legislature of the State of Wyoming

A RESOLUTION recognizing the 65th Wedding Anniversary of Jake and Martha Korell by the Wyoming State Senate.

WHEREAS, Jake and Martha united on March 9th, 1936 and were the first couple to be married in the Lutheran Church at Torrington, Wyoming;

WHEREAS, this Resolution has the support of the members of the Senate of the Wyoming Legislature who have signed their names hereto.

Now, Therefore, Be It Resolved By the Undersigned Members of the Senate of the Legislature of the State of Wyoming:

Section 1. That Jake and Martha's service to their community and the State of Wyoming is exemplary.

Section 2. That Jake and Martha's dedication to each other sets an example for all our citizens that is acknowledged and applauded by all the members of the 56th Wyoming Legislature.

Therefore, with great appreciation, we recognize Jake and Martha for their outstanding dedication and support to each other and to the State of Wyoming this 1st day of March 2001.

Henry H.R. "Hank" Coe
President of the Senate

Jake was the 7th inductee to the National Trappers Hall of Fame.

A Tribute
to
Aunt Martha & Uncle Jake

65 years ago a fellow named JAKE
Convinced young MARTHA a good husband he'd make.
Nebraska is where they tied the knot
Changing their minds, and any price, could not be bought

Later a move to Wyoming to their home on the range
A sparsely settled area, quite a change
The land, undeveloped, near what is now known as Kinnear
Where they lived in quiet except for occasional coyotes they'd hear

While nestled on this farm scarcely cleared of sagebrush
Times then how different from today's "rush, rush, rush"
During this time, God chose the to be graciously blessed
Along came Lee Roy, Jane, and Jerry to join their nest

Time and memory elude me and I don't remember when they made the change
They relocated nearer Riverton and left their home on the range
In Riverton "Korell Quarter Horse" became their home's new name
Where they ran 60-70 prancing horses, not wild but tame

These stallions and mares branded "Flying Quarter circle Lazy DV"
Were as sleek and high-spirited as any you'd see
They never lost sight of who they were or where they were going
Always meeting the next challenge – reaping what they were sowing

Working the land in sunshine and rain
And tending the livestock produced steady gain
A heart-breaking disease beset son, Lee Roy
Their oldest child who'd never be a Wyoming cowboy

He was stricken with polio, a 1950's epidemic widespread
Which brought terror and fear and oh! So much dread
In spite of disability, he graduated as an accountant and worked as a 'pro"
The problems and difficulties he experienced, we'll never know

We pay tribute to him with all of our love
As the Good Lord wanted Lee to be with Him above
But in site of your grieving and sorrow, his loss brought much pain
You weathered the storm and with Divine help, carried on despite the strain

Assisting in this recovery were daughter, Jan and son, Jerry
Both helping to make your lives so much more merry
And with these two jewels your family grew
Adding Scott, and Iva, and talented Kathy too

And isn't it wonderful to have them nearby
In reality it's like your "pie in the sky"
With Jane and Scott a stone's throw away—just next door
Available when needed to help with a chore

The same is true of Iva and Jerry and Kathy albeit temporarily
Since she's in college and seen more rarely
But, oh what joy to her parents and grandparents she brings
The ambitious young lady has really taken off – soaring on wings

We must reflect a bit on housewife, Aunt Martha and trapper, Uncle Jake
What a congenial, happy couple they make
She helped on the farm and I know she's thinned beets
Leaving that hard work was one of her treats

That doesn't mean, however, her hard work had ended
It just changed to other duties which her time it demanded
And during this time she amassed a lovely antique collection
Which prompts one to pause a moment for reflection

Of the many aged heirlooms from the good of past
Here's hoping the legacy from the preceding century will long last
I know of no one with Uncle Jake's stamina, experience, talent and strength
When it comes to hunting, trapping, fishing and stories of any length

It's not by accident he was select to the "Trapper's Hall of Fame"
Its because of the knowledge, wisdom, expertise, and "moxie" behind his name
He's a real solid genuine Man of the West, strong as steel
The Native American accepted him as one of them, not a fake but real.

We can't forget the "Rendezvous" in which he regularly takes part
Joining the Indians and others, he really takes this to heart
Beating the drums he personally handcrafted from his work as a trapper
I'm sure he prefers "hya, hya" music with his drums to that of a Hollywood
"rapper"

"Behind every successful man is a devoted woman" as the saying goes
He couldn't have done it without Aunt Martha, I think he knows

As hard-working Germans they've been a real success
How could we have expected anything less

And together they've lived an exciting and colorful life
As a committed, adventurous team known as 'husband and wife'

Congratulations! To Aunt Martha and Uncle Jake –two people my family and I hold very dear –They have experienced and endured as much together as they complete their 65th year

With much love,
Your niece Dorothy Bogrett, Daughter Becky,
son Blake and family

BARJO AND THE HEIFER

By Terry Angel

The neighbors had a Holstein heifer.
She wasn't nothin' fancy.
But about the time she turned three,
She started I' sort of antsy.

They tried to work with her a little.
The more they did, the more she got contrary,
So they said, "The Hell with it;
We'll sell her to the dairy!"

They decided to run her in one day.
She was with the bunch in the back forty.
'It took 'em quite some time, you see,
'Cause man, she was I' snorty.

They got her in the corral,
And ran her up the chute,
All the time a thinkin',
Boy, it'll be nice to be rid of this beaut.

They finally had her captured,
So happy about their good luck,
But hell, they should have known,
She wasn't gonna stay in that there truck.

To say she was excited,
Wouldn't be pushin' it one little dab.
Once she got her front feet over,
That heifer left via the cab.

This may sound kind of crazy,
But this is where it gets interestin',
'Cause I'll tell you that spring,
She caused 'em to do one helluva bunch of fencin'.

She headed down toward Eighth Street,
As if she were Devil sent.
She came up against eleven fences,
That she either jumped, or broke or bent.

When she got in with Jerry's cows,
She calmed enough to get her feet on the ground.
The neighbors all breathed a sigh of relief,
'Cause things sure had been lookin' down.

Things might be lookin' up, with a little cowboy help.
Ya see, the place was on now belonged to Jerry Korell.
Everyone knew he had a real nice black,
And three or four good sorrels.

The heathen was content with those cows,
So Jerry said with a cough,
As hard as that old gal's been workin',
Maybe we ought to give her the rest of the day off."

They started afresh in the mornin',
To run the loco critter on in.
This is where Jerry discovered,
That cow was just damned hard to pen.

When she went through the side of the corral,
Jerry was starting to get pissed.
He went to the barn for his rope,
And saddled up BarJo Twist.

She proceeded to tear out the fences,
So Jerry fell in behind at a lope,
And around the neck of this crazed bitch from hell,
He threw his lariat rope.

He started to drag her to the corral,
But she must have weighed twelve hundred pounds.
He fell in behind to drive her,
But she thought him and his horse were the Hounds.[2]

She spun around to face them.
I don't need to say she was mad, of course.
She blew snot and threw mud, and with a helluva lunge,
She run plum under his horse.

Jerry's dad, Jake, was up by the barn,
When he discovered his son in distress.
He jumped on his Allis Chalmers,
And headed out to help clean up the mess.

[2] Hounds from Hell

As Jake raced across the field to help him,
Jerry had just about given up hope.
He got his lariat free and let go,
When Jake slid to a stop, right on the rope.

The cow had a new enemy now.
She thought the tractor was a foe to be beat.
Or maybe she thought it was a means of escape,
'Cause she chased Jake right out of his seat.

Jake's up on top of the tractor,
Hollerin', kickin' and screamin'.
Jerry races to get another rope,
In hopes of controllin' this demon.

They threw one more rope upon her,
Tied her hard and fast to the drawbar,
Fired up that Allis Chalmers,
And drug her fast and far.

Once in the corral, they tied her to a post,
Then went and got the horse trailer,
Backed it up and loaded her,
All the time cussin' her like a sailor.

Now she's tryin' to kick her way out of the trailer.
Jerry's really I' hot.
He hauled her down to Doc McLean,
Said, "Give this bitch a shot."

He heads out to the dairy;
She's still destined to be a milk cow.
Jerry all the time athinkin',
I'd rather milk a sow.

He got her there and turned her loose.
She landed atop the fence, at escaping she was slick.
Ran right through the milk cow herd,
Last seen headed for 5 Mile Creek.

That wild heifer was rounded up again.
And loaded into the horse trailer some how
Went straight to Riverton Auction this time.
Someone enjoyed hamburger from her now.

PROFILE OF A TRAPPER

Trapper Jake

Jake Korell, now 90, is enjoying his 83rd year on the trapline. Energetic and spry for a man half his age, Jake is a well-known trapper in Wyoming. In spite of the fact Jake Korell was one of the seven original inductees in the NTA Hall of Fame; he may be one of the least nationally known members of this prestigious honor.

But just say Trapper Jake around Riverton, Wyoming and most everyone smiles as Jake has been around promoting trapping and participating in any event that promotes furs for many years. Korell has trained many trappers during his lifetime including a number of professional trappers still working today.

One of Jake's many contributions to this community is the donation of a complete set of Newhouse traps and a large collection of mounted furbearers and big game animals. This collection is on display at the Wind River Heritage Center, a free museum of natural history frequented by local folks and tourists alike. All the animals in this display were taken and mounted by Jake and his son Jerry, who continues to do taxidermy work for the hunting community.

Born in Nebraska, Jake Korell moved with his family to Goshen County, Wyoming as a toddler. During his first two years of trapping as a seven and eight-year old, Jake managed to catch between 20 and 30 muskrats. They sold for $1 to $1.25 each at that time, which added to the funds to help raise the family of nine children. Jake's third season specialized mostly on skunks because they were worth something, and the added value was he was often dismissed from school soon after arrival in the morning.

By Jane Maller

Korell moved to the Riverton, Wyoming area in 1936. He discovered he had a natural ability as a boxer, so the story goes he was known to get in a little fight once in a while with or without gloves. In addition to farming, he hired out to trap predators for local ranchers. Jake soon gathered quite a reputation with his skills and determination. While trapping on the local Griffin ranch at age 65, Mr. Griffin observed that Jake walked 40 miles one day, ending his journey at 11 p.m. that evening.

Even in recent years, Trapper Jake still maintains sizable traplines for coyotes, beaver, fox, bobcats and everything else worth a buck. His catches are wonderful. He almost always takes more than 100 coyotes during a season, running his traps two days in a row, then skinning the third. A retired rancher and trapper, Leonard Gradert, has partnered up with Jake for this season. If he has trouble, we are certain Jake will

Trapper Jake outside the fur barn with a day's catch in November, 2002. Totals for the day included six coyotes, a beaver and a cat.

Korrell with a huge sagebrush tom taken on the prairie.

There is no mistaking Jake in his familiar beaver hat and badger coat. He is one of a kind, uniquely skilled; and he has earned the respect of his community.

told Jake they had to run him to jail for trespassing. Jake said simply, "No, you ain't." The wardens asked the old trapper why he was so sure. Jake replied. "Cuz there's only two of you."

They left laughing so hard they could barely get in their pickup truck.

Bets around here are Jake was right.

Trapping has been a major love and accomplishment in Jake Korell's life. He is still known to be able to walk a young man into the ground; and when they pick on his age, he is likely to say, "I'll probably be at your funeral too."

Now and then someone might take a look at the NTA list of Hall of Fame members and wonder who Jake Korell is. Jake Korell is a trapper's trapper. He has helped folks in need for many years with his trapping skills. He has helped many young trappers learn great ways to set traps and handle furs right. His catches draw envy from all trappers, young or not so young, close and far.

He has always been generous with his time and contributions to the local community. Trapper Jake makes you proud.——**Jane Maller**, Riverton, WY 82501.

carry him home for any necessary medical treatments.

Jake has made his own lures for years. He may sell you a bottle or give you a bottle or not. It depends a lot on whether he thinks you are good enough to appreciate something special.

There is a story around this western cow town that a few years back Jake's hounds got to trailing a varmint and drifted off on the trail toward Indian reservation land. Jake was chasing his dogs when he was approached by two Native American game wardens who

Top L-R 1. Jake Korell's Great Grandmother, Dorthea Elizabeth (Stenzel) Wagner, taken shortly after her arrival in Russell, KS, from Russia in 1903. She was approximately 67 years old. She was born 7/6/1836 in Sarepta, Russia, and died 5/19/1920 and is buried in Russell, Kansas

2. Jake's Father, Pvt. Heinrich Jaconlich Korell, 144. Kamchatka Regiment, 9th Company, Russia, circa 1906

3. J 3. Jake Korell's Great, Great Grandmother and Great, Great Grandfather, Johannes Stenzel and Anna Margarete (Sitzmann) Stenzel, taken before 1878 in Russia. Johannes was born 12/4/1810 in Sarepta, Russia, and was buried 10/11/1878 at Frank, Russia, at age 67. Anna was born 6/2/1814 in Frank, Russia, and died 5/25/1894 at Saratov, Russia, at age 80.

4. Jake Korell's Parents, Elizabeth (Ernst) Korell and Heinrich "Henry" Jaconlich Korell, taken in 1912 in Lingle, Wyoming.

Jake's Ancestors

Right—Jake's grandmother (wearing headscarf) Anna Maria Sophia Katherine (Wagner) Ernst and family. Anna Marie was born 9/18/1955 in Carpet, Russia, and was buried 1/11/37 in Mitchell, Nebraska, at the age of 81. Picture taken in Russell, Kansas, about 1919, when she was approximately 55 years of age.

98

Korell Family

Lee was a brilliant accountant and handled the paperwork for Jake Korell and Sons Fur. He had a keen interest in trapping, even though he couldn't actually run his own trap line because of his polio. He helped Jake build a fine trap collection until he died.

Jerry has followed in his father's footsteps: trapping, buying fur, doing taxidermy work and raising outstanding quarter horses. He excels at everything he does and has gained wide respect for his knowledge and expertise in all of the above-mentioned areas. In 1962 Jerry joined the family business. He increased the fur buying venture and included tanning and taxidermy facilities. They outfitted and guide hunters. They rode and broke many broncs, and a common statement often overheard was, "If Jake or Jerry can't ride 'em, no one can!" His wife, Iva, helps with the fur business and has taken over the paperwork since Lee's death.

Jane went to Casper College and received an Associate of Arts degree. She manages the Center's gift shop. Jane married Scott Maller, a Wyoming rancher and welder, and they reside near Jake's ranch. They enjoy going on hunting and fishing pack-trips with Jake and family.

Jerry and Iva's daughter, Kathy, is an accomplished horsewoman and has won numerous rodeo awards. She is currently attending graduate school.

WIND RIVER HERITAGE CENTER
EDUCATIONAL TRUNK CONTENTS

In the above picture Jake Korell is teaching about the mountain men. He is using the trap display at the Heritage center as well as a traveling trunk that can be checked out by any school group or organization.

The trunk contains:

1. Videos

        (a) Rocky Mountain Beaver Pond (1 copy)
        (b) Lewis & Clark "Journey West" (1 copy)
        (c) Lewis & Clark "How we Cross the West" (2 copies)
        (d) Adventure of Joe Meek "River of the West (1 copy)

2. Clothing

        (a) Capote
        (b) Hats (2) High top/ Flat & round hat
        (c) Shirt
        (d) Elk-Skin Trousers

(e) Leather Belt (made from harness strap)

(f) Buffalo-Hide Moccasins

(g) Deerskin Ladies' Moccasins

3. Possibles Bag

(a) Fire Starting Kit

(b) Sewing Kit

(c) Bag of Bullets

(d) Peace/ Parlay or Friendship Pipe

4. Parfleche Case that would usually would contain salt, flour, sugar, beans, coffee, rice, jerky, etc.

5. Package of Sample Hair: Moose, Antelope, Bear, Mountain Sheep, Buffalo.

6. Animal Traps:

(a) Size 4 Coyote, Beaver, Mountain Lion, Wolf, Bobcat Trap

(b) Size 3 Raccoon, Fox, Beaver, Coyote Trap

(c) Size 2 Mink, Otter, Skunk Trap

(d) Size 1 Muskrat, Pine Marten Trap

7. Pelts

(a) 1 Quality Beaver Plew

(b) 1 Coyote Hide

(c) 1 Ermine Hide

(d) Beaver Castor Container (beaver bait)

(e) 1 Pine Marten (Sable) Hide

(f) 1 Raccoon Hide

8. Armaments:

(a) Green River – type knife

(b) Skinning knife

(c) Hawk or Tomahawk

(d) Stone War Club

(e) Powder Horn

(f) Deerskin Rifle Case

(g) Monarch

(h) 45 Caliber Cap lock, Muzzle-Loading, Black Powder Rifle, Serial Number G4682

(i) Indian Bow with 1 Arrow in Parfleche Case

9. Miscellaneous items: Indian-type Halter/Bridle